T0128940

Some Governance and Peaceful Coexistence Issues for Sustainable Advancement

A Nigerian Perspective

A. W. Lawrence

authorHOUSE®

AuthorHouse™
1663 Liberty Drive
Bloomington, IN 47403
www.authorhouse.com
Phone: 1 (800) 839-8640

Published by AuthorHouse 01/08/2018

ISBN: 978-1-5462-2143-2 (sc)
ISBN: 978-1-5462-2142-5 (hc)
ISBN: 978-1-5462-2141-8 (e)

Library of Congress Control Number: 2017919092

All Bible Verses are taken from KJV

To the future generations of human beings, especially Nigerians.

Foreword

Nigeria is currently passing through a period of protracted stress in its journey towards sustainable development as a nation. Glaring manifestations of governance failures dot the social and economic landscape, and there is a growing and palpable dissatisfaction among large swathes of its populace. Civil servants complain over delays in paying their salaries; the budgeting process is characterized by huge time overruns, by indiscipline, and by the phenomenon of padding, something which, were it not simply a crying scandal and shame, would have won Nigeria a place of honour in the halls of fame for farce and the tragicomic. Interethnic clashes with fatalities are on the rise, the most worrisome being those between nomadic pastoralists and farming populations. Religiously driven clashes are on the rise too, and the ensuing instabilities and distrust they create continue to frustrate any efforts at national cohesion building. Corruption remains a key challenge and a deterrent to true national development, and even efforts to address it have been marred by demonstrable instances of selectivity and score settling in targeting. The symptoms of dysfunction are there for all to see, the most glaring illustrations being the resurgence of ethnically driven centrifugal clamours and calls for restructuring.

This is the context and environment in which this wonderful and easily readable book by Sir Anthony Wakwe Lawrence, *Some Governance and Peaceful Coexistence Issues for Sustainable Advancement: A Nigerian Perspective*, is written. The book is an X-ray of some of the social and political issues facing Nigeria, carried out by a man who is clearly sad that his country is underperforming and has constantly failed to live up to its potential and promise. The book is made up of seven chapters of unequal lengths, with chapter 4 being the longest, and overflows with a great deal of sombre realism in its descriptions of instances of governance and other failures in Nigeria. The methodological approach adopted in the book is a blend of history, sociology, and political science that leans towards functionalist interpretations.

Chapter 1 takes the reader on an excursion into the origins of human societies and on how and why societies evolved from simple to complex societies. Essentially, simple societies evolved into larger ones because of the need for safety, the conquest and absorption of weaker units by stronger ones, consolidation of earlier disparate units, and the demands for specialization within the emergent and larger structures. Rules, roles, and responsibilities were then crafted and shared out to ensure the survival and smooth running of these new units, with the right levels of rewards and incentives always provided to ensure their continued smooth running.

Chapter 2 examines the origins of present-day Nigeria, and Sir Lawrence devotes some time to pointing to the existence and flourishing of large kingdoms and empires in precolonial Nigeria, though Sir Lawrence, largely because of the brevity of this chapter, misses the opportunity to let his reader know whether some of the ills of present day were also in existence in the precolonial societies that make it up. This same chapter examines the Nigerian Civil War; the post-conflict period; the era of the military; and their unending capacity for coups and counter-coups right up to the adoption, some would say imposition, of the 1999 constitution. The chapter discusses the Ogoni crisis, a crisis whose ripples continue to be felt up till in present day Nigeria in the voices of environmentalists and resource control proponents. The number of issues treated in this chapter sadly prevents Sir Lawrence from examining some of them in any detail. Despite the brevity, however, two things emerge as one gets to the end of the chapter—Sir Lawrence's nostalgia for the old regional arrangements, his dislike for the military imposed unitarist structures, and his leaning towards those who argue for some form of restructuring.

Chapter 3 presents a theoretical model on the evolution of human societies and their political structures—most readers will find this engaging, as Sir Lawrence posits an eight-level (eight-phase system) in political evolution, with jungle justice being at the base and service at the top. According to Sir Lawrence, societies evolve from jungle politics to religious politics to ethnic politics to power politics to democracy to politics of inclusiveness to politics of ideas and, finally, to politics of service. Sir Anthony Wakwe Lawrence laments the fact that present-day Nigeria manifests aspects of all eight levels and ends this chapter pleading for a moral reorientation to get us moving forward.

Chapter 4 is the chapter where the writer pours out his soul and his angst at the numerous social ills that afflict Nigeria. The chapter is broad-ranging and covers about eighteen distinct topics—zoning and federal character, rule of law, impunity, revenue generation, indolence, women's empowerment, superstition and ritualism, education for all, relevant education, Almajiri education and educational imbalance, role of competition, national development goals and priorities, subsidies and cash transfer programmes for youths, management of fuel subsidy projects, sycophancy, mismanaging communication, rumours and gossips, improving our electoral practices, religion and ethnic terrorism, and homosexuality—a huge serving indeed, all written with passion and boldness. Sir Anthony Wakwe Lawrence says it the way he sees and feels it. He is speaking his mind, and he does not always expect the reader to agree with him. The author does not pull his punches, and he often abandons all diplomacy and efforts at social correctness as he slams into positions that he does not believe in—be it witchcraft, ethnic terrorism, or homosexuality. My take is that this chapter should have been broken into two separate chapters and a way found to sequence the numerous topics within it.

Chapter 5 is on conflict and is treated in a style, manner, depth, sensitivity, and practicality that reflect Sir Lawrence's many years of professional engagement as a community liaison officer and community development officer, Eastern Operations of Shell Petroleum Company, Port Harcourt. Sir Anthony Lawrence, who was on my team when I led the Community Development Planning and Delivery Team for

SPDC, is at pains to point out the dangers of conflict and is able to propose models that, if followed, would allow persons and groups to step in the other's shoes and, thus, begin to appreciate their points of view. Embedded in Sir Anthony Wakwe Lawrence's exploration in this chapter are the concepts of empathy, collaboration, cooperation, complementing, compromise, and communication, the absence of which are the roots of most conflicts. The chapter is rich in quotes, which reflects Sir Anthony's many years in peace-building work. Here is just one of such: 'When arrogance, anger, and intolerance colour a conflict, belligerence, violence, and regrets all become the expected set of reference outcomes.'

The reader will also find in this chapter a number of useful models and graphical representations of conflict, conflict resolution, and constructive engagement.

Chapter 6 is on sustainable development, sustainable advancement, population, and the environment. It examines the whole population, environment, and development dynamics, including the concept of carrying capacity, sustainable use, and the triple bottom lines of people, profits, and planet that have become so important in development thinking since the Cairo and Rio conferences on population and environment respectively in the nineties. It is a chapter that is worth reading with attention, especially since it uses some of the flashpoints of Nigeria to illustrate a number of the issues of development of global concern.

Chapter 7 examines corruption and other matters arising, though I had wished that Sir Anthony had remained focused solely on corruption in this chapter. Apart from this reservation and the fact that Sir Anthony focuses largely on punitive means to deal with corruption, I find this final chapter to be a useful one. Sir Anthony brings in a very important quote is this chapter, which bears repeating here: 'Let us know that any society or organization that resists change by all means also insists on stagnation and eventual decline by any means.'

Sir Anthony has written a very readable and useful book. Development practitioners and conflict resolution experts will find many portions of it very useful. They will like the broad span of knowledge from which it draws—sociology, psychology, economics, history, geography, and culture. They will find his sharing of his years of experience both unpatronizing and calming. I am sure that they will find some freshness in some of Sir Anthony's bold assertions and, hopefully, have the resilience to absorb the shock of some heavy assertions that he occasionally puts across to his readers. For example, he writes, 'Democracy encourages mediocrity. Don't get offended because that is the truth.' On that note, I now invite the reader to join me and other readers in this feast of ideas and, having feasted, to apply our learning creatively and constructively to contribute to good governance and peaceful coexistence wherever we may find ourselves.

Dr Noel Anyalemachi Ihebuzor
Onye nkuzi Nnaze
Abuja

Acknowledgements

I will start by thanking my God, who gave me the gifts, the patience with the persistent zeal not to give up, the opportunity, the experience, and the life without which this book would not have been written.

I thank my wife, Dame Dr Barasua Anthony Lawrence for the support and love. Her presence in my life has been rewarding, and I am grateful to her for the good upbringing and support she gave to my five children (Dango, Damiete, Owanari, Orolobo, and Anthonia).

I thank my sisters and brothers, especially Mrs Christiana Briggs, Pastor Mrs Boma Patricia Jack Umah, and Chief Professor Victor Chukwuma Wakwe for the love they have shown to me. I am proud of my family and the brotherly love we share.

I must remember my late mum, Madam Elfrida D. Manuel, who sacrificed a lot to see me become what I am today. I also will not forget the love that exists within my extended families and the care I enjoyed from my uncles (the late Honourable Justice MacGregor Manuel, Mr D. R. Bob Manuel, and Mr Mangibo Ekine, among others); aunties; nephews and nieces; cousins; and in-laws.

I must thank my friends for making life enjoyable, and some of them have been like brothers and sisters. I equally thank those friends who I have shared some of my thoughts with over the years, for the comments and criticisms I have received through the period were of great help in the making of this book.

I am grateful to my first son, Dango Lawrence; his management of our non-governmental organization (Community Inter-Relations and

Conciliation Initiative [CIRCI]) has helped me to carry other things on board.

I again thank my second son, Damiete Lawrence (Loxxy), who believed and advised persistently that it was time I wrote a book and gave me all moral encouragement while it was being written. Damiete, Dame Dr Mercy Oke-Chinda, and Dr Noel Ihebuzor provided invaluable editorial support, using their time, energy, and intellect. God bless you.

Contents

1

Some Perspectives on the Evolution of Large Societies

There are several accounts on how humans emerged into existence from creation. Every religion has its account, and science has an account it prefers to stand by. One thing, however, that is not controvertible is that humankind has been changing and is continually changing, not only in its adaptive attributes to surviving in the environment but also in its ideas as humanity expands its horizon of knowledge.

Humankind's evolutionary attributes have affected all aspects of humanity. Humans must have been living in solitary entities with close family units at the early stages of human existence on the earth. They fended for food and protected themselves from wild beasts and from other human neighbours. These small units must have been exposed to numerous hazards, such as attacks by other predators and wars from other expansionist human units. Life must have been short, brutish, and unpredictable.

In my mind, two things may have encouraged communal living. When a human unit engages another unit in war, the winner may choose both to kill the threats in the captured group (men) and then to take over its other members as slaves into its own unit. Alternatively, communal living may come about by related units coming together to form a stronger unit that can repel or overcome enemies.

Either approach over time will lead to an increase in the size of these emergent units, and leadership will be required to ensure that such units—or now societies—function well in protecting these emerging societies against all forms of enemies. In most of such societies, leaders who are the most powerful and who can fight and kill all others will be instinctively feared and obeyed by everyone else, and in each case, this person will also engage lieutenants who will help in the administration of such units.

The survival of the units and the leader then becomes the primary responsibility of the leader. It follows that, as societies evolve, people will have to take up responsibilities of protection, of farming and hunting for food, of education, of appeasing the gods, and so on.

That is the evolution of specialization, where people in societies devote time to acquiring skills in order to provide services in the society.

Specialization is critical for a working society, since it enables people to devote time to learning and to research; this is because many people depend on those who do so for the provision of such services. Thanks to such specializations, native doctors or medical doctors, house builders, spiritualists, soldiers, administrators, and others all become proficient in their fields of endeavour in a bid to retain their patrons.

The evolution of communal living did not start with humans. Even bacteria live in colonies. Kindly permit me to refer to the Bible, which recognizes the wisdom of the ants who are able to prepare for the winter in the summer; this scripture can be found in Proverbs 30:25. Again in Proverbs 6:6, the Bible advised humankind to go to the ant, consider its ways, and be wise. The ants have specialization within their population. They have the soldiers, the workers, the queen, and so on. Communal living is common among many wild beasts, including lions, antelopes, and many more. Many animals (birds, fishes, wild mammals) by instinct come together and journey together to procreate. That indicates the importance of staying together for the survival of the species.

Specialization also ensures teamwork, since everyone depends on one another for life sustenance. As societies continue to evolve, those societies that had wise rulers, encouraged enterprise, and rewarded ingenuity began to advance faster than those that enslaved everyone. With time, weaker societies and kingdoms would be overrun by greater kingdoms.

Humanity has had great kingdoms, and great kingdoms have been destroyed by greater kingdoms. The game has remained the survival of the fittest.

One thing we must not lose sight of is the role of science in the rapid advancement of societies. While some societies actively encouraged scientific pursuits by providing incentives for scientific breakthroughs, others (because of conservatism and superstition) actively fought against scientific changes. It is true that even in modern days, some societies, for inexplicable reasons, may still discourage scientific findings that go contrary to their current beliefs, could alter their ways of life, or make their current means of livelihood redundant or outdated.

Despite all that I have said in terms of the role of security and specialization in the advancement of virile societies, every progressive society must have effective laws and customs to ensure a peaceful and harmonious society where everyone is happy. That means that the rulers must put in place the dos and don'ts—and also put in place penalties for defaulters. Such a set of laws and regulations would help in caging in the antisocial elements that would tend to disrupt the smooth running of such society. A society without guiding principles will be in anarchy, and impunity will reign.

2

Some Perspectives on the Evolution of the Nigerian Nation

Numerous ethnic nations have occupied the Nigerian geographical space. They range from the Hausa, the Bornu, and other kingdoms situated from the Niger River to Lake Chad. Some of these ethnic nations existed before 11,000 BC. The existence of communities like Iwo-Eleru in the south-west and Ugwelle-Uturu (Okigwe) in the south-east since that time is documented (Leonard 2009; Jones 2001).

According to the same sources, the Fulani entered Hausa land around the thirteenth century, and by the fifteenth century they were already within the Kanem-Bornu land spaces. The report also stated that, although the vast majority of the inhabitants of the area were Muslim by the sixteenth century, they were attacked by Fulani jihadists from 1804 to 1808; by 1808, the Hausa Nation was conquered by Usman dan Fodio and brought under the rule of Sokoto Caliphate.[7]

The Yoruba people, on the other hand, are found in the south-western part of Nigeria. They are the main group on the western side of the Niger, occupying many city states. Their nearest relatives, the Igala, live on the opposite side, where the Niger River meets the Benue River.

The Igbos are the majority tribe of the south-eastern part of Nigeria. Igboland, like the Yoruba, has many city states. There are the Akwa city state, the Onitsha kingdoms, and the Umunoha state in the Owerri area, among many.

Nigeria is said to have more than 450 tribes who were more or less independent ethnic nations prior to British colonialism. Apart from the three major tribes of Hausa, Yoruba, and Igbos, there are many other tribes, including the Ijaws, who mainly live in the coastal parts and riverbanks within the Niger Delta region. There are many other minority tribes within the Nigerian territory.

There are diverse beliefs by the various ethnic groups on their origins and how their ethnic groups came into existence.

Some states and kingdoms that existed prior to British colonialism include:

- Benin Kingdom
- Borgu Kingdom
- Fulani Empire
- Hausa Kingdoms
- Ibani
- Kalabari
- Kanem Bornu Empire
- Kwararafa Kingdom
- Ibibio Kingdom
- Nembe Kingdom
- Nri Kingdom
- Nupe Kingdom
- Ogbia Kingdom
- Oyo Empire
- Songhai Empire
- Warri Kingdom

These are just a few of many, totalling more than four hundred ethnic nations (Sule 2014; Leonard 2009; Jones 2001).

Britain, along with other European countries, scrambled to possess Africa. Nigeria was eventually taken by Britain. The British came with the intention to explore and exploit the resources of the nation for their own good. First it was to acquire slaves, who would make up a cheap workforce in their own nation. They knew that, if their intention was clean, all they needed to do was to negotiate with the communities and parents on how their children could go over to Britain (for example) to work for an agreed sum and choose to return home when they so desired. Rather, they chose to acquire people by force through slave merchants who stole people and sold them to the British merchants. The acquired slaves were treated as subhuman for the sole purpose of maximizing the merchants' productivity. Many died during their transportation; many were stolen as children; and many died in foreign lands, where they begot several generations of slaves. Slave children were considered in the same way we consider domestic animals, and offspring of slaves were slaves themselves. They had no future plans of their own, since they were the property of the slave owner. By the time the slave trade was abolished, these people no longer knew their roots and, therefore, became citizens of Britain or any other country they were in. Some chose to return to Africa and settled in places like Liberia.

Let me also say that some Britons and others saw the colonization as an opportunity to spread the 'good news' of Jesus Christ, and as a result, they were able to convert many Nigerians into Christians.

Nigeria was also exploited for other resources in the form of trade. Our agricultural produce fed the booming industries in Britain. Though this was a fairer trade (our nation earned some foreign exchange from the business, as we sold cocoa, groundnuts, oil palm, and other resources) I would think that we earned less than what our products were worth since it was more or less a monopolistic relationship.

Later came crude oil production and sale.

Nigeria became a British protectorate on 1 January 1901. At that time in world history, Britain was the most powerful nation in the entire world.

Within fourteen years, by 1914, Britain had amalgamated the colonies and protectorates into one administrative unit. Despite these efforts, Nigeria remained divided into the northern and southern Provinces and Lagos Colony. With persistent demand for independence by Nigerian nationalists, the British government made Nigeria an autonomous federation on 1 October 1954. On 1 October 1960, Britain gave independence to the nation of Nigeria.

This new nation adopted parliamentary government like its former colonialist government, with three regions each having substantial self-governance.

This government was headed by Sir Abubakar Tafawa Belewa, who was the prime minister, and Nnamdi Azikiwe was the ceremonial president of the nation.

At the regional levels, the following were premiers—in the north, Ahmadu Bello, the Saduana of Sokoto; in the west, Chief Obafemi Awolowo; and in the east, Dr Michael Okpara.

The unfortunate event of coup on 15 January 1966 by some young majors led by Major Kaduna Nzeogwu, mainly from the Igbo stock, massively derailed the already bad situation. Sir Abubakar Tafawa Belewa and the then premiers of northern and western regions, namely Ahmadu Bello and Samuel Akintola respectively, among others, were killed.

This coup was frustrated, and a military government headed by General Johnson Aguiyi-Ironsi emerged from it. This first military government became a unitary government, as expected, with the highest and unquestionable command system from the head of state, who ruled by promulgating decrees. The failed coup and the fact that the new head of state was from the Igbo stock, whose tribe contributed the bulk that carried out the coup, aggravated the conflict, and many Igbos in the north were killed in a pogrom. This conflict eventually resulted in a counter-coup that took the lives of General Aguyi-Ironsi and Colonel Adekule Fajuyi, who was hosting the then head of state.

Eventually a full-scale civil war started when the Igbos, led by Colonel Odumegwu Ojukwu declared independence from Nigeria as Biafra.

The war ended when representatives of Biafra conceded victory to the Nigerian military government led by General Yakubu Gowon in 1970. However, this war cost Biafra many lives, mainly from actual war casualties and from starvation.

This war did not only impact negatively on the Igbos; many minorities within the south-eastern part of Nigeria and some in the midwest region suffered casualties, despite the fact that a good number

7

of them did not see themselves as Igbos or Biafra. They were afraid that, because they were minorities, the Igbos would not treat them well. This positioning by some minorities, especially the Kalabari people, who are Ijaws, resulted in their ill treatment by the Biafran army. The army maltreated those they considered as saboteurs, and many were killed in Abonnema (a Kalabari land). Eventually for whatever reason, the Biafran army chose to evacuate all of the Kalabari communities, starting with Abonnema and Bakana. However, these communities were lucky, as the Nigerian army overcame them just as they were being evacuated, and the Kalabari ethnic nation was liberated from this sinister intention of the Biafran army.

In societies where impunity is norm, majority groups will first of all take care of their own interests before considering others, especially minorities, and this affects weak minorities more because they have less power or voice to demand justice. The minorities in the Niger Delta of Nigeria where the crude oil is produced are still not getting the best of deals from the Nigerian nation after the civil war.

Several events happened after the cessation of the civil war. General Yakubu Gowon continued as head of state, and he ruled for about nine years, always postponing the return to civilian regime. Then on 29 July 1975, General Murtala Mohammed staged a coup that overthrew General Gowon. General Murtala Mohammed was assassinated in an unsuccessful coup, leading the way for Lieutenant General Olusegun Obasanjo to take over as head of state.

General Obasanjo handed over power to a civilian regime, with Alhaji Shehu Shagari as the president of the nation. This military regime headed by General Obasanjo facilitated the new constitution that was used by the new civilian regime. As expected, some of the issues in the constitution had not been subjected to any serious review or deliberations. This failure was made even worse by the fact that members of the constitution drafting committee had approached their task with a poorly concealed military mentality, resulting in a constitution with a strong leaning towards a unitary system of government that was the hallmark of the soldiers. Again, at this time, many Nigerians were used to the easy money coming from sales of crude oil from the minority sections of the nation, and the unitary system was ideal to own and use the revenue the way the central government wished.

The civilian second term only lasted a little more than one year, when General Mohammadu Buhari struck and terminated it on 31 December 1983, ending the opportunity for learning through civilian mass action and resistance to stop the continued mismanagement of governance through electoral malpractices, corruption, and impunity.

However, by this time, the coup bug had bitten Nigeria, and the overthrow of governments became very frequent. General Ibrahim Babangida overthrew Major General Muhammadu Buhari in August 1985.

General Babangida tried a number of policies and experimented on how to introduce good civilian governance. Some were actually promising, like the option A4, where voting was open, as voters queued behind the picture of their candidates to be counted and so forth. However, he was instrumental to his disgraceful ousting, as he annulled the election that was acclaimed to have been won by M. K. O. Abiola. The mass agitations by Nigerians were unbearable, and he had to hand over power to Ernest Shonekan, who headed an interim government from 27 August 1993. Ernest Shonekan did not last long, as a member of his cabinet, General Sani Abacha (then Defence Minister), forced him to resign and became the head of state on 17 November 1993.

Consequent upon the annulment of the 12 June election, many nations severed their ties with Nigeria, and the embargo worsened our already deplorable economic situation.

Eventually Moshood Kashimawo Olawale Abiola, who declared himself president, was arrested, and he died in prison.

General Abacha's regime was plagued with so many unpleasant issues. General Obasanjo and Major General YarAdua were accused of planning a coup and were jailed. YarAdua died in prison.

Vanguard, the newspaper based in Lagos, reported that there was violence across Ogoni land as a result of demand for Ogoni Bill of Rights resulting in the killing of Albert Badey, Edwin Kobani, Samuel Orage, and Theophilus Orage at Gokoo in Gokana Local Government

Area on 21 May 1993. This eventually led to the prosecution and conviction of Ken Sarowiwa (a prominent activist) and eight others by a special tribunal set up to adjudicate Ogoni civil disturbances. Most people were not happy with the action of General Abacha's government, because the accused persons were not availed the right of appeal.

Many prominent politicians were murdered by unknown people during Abacha's era. The wife of Chief M. K. O. Abiola, among others, was assassinated.

General Abacha died, and this brought that era to an end. General Abdulsalami Abubakar, who took over from him on 8 June 1998, committed to civilian rule again. The fourth civilian republic came to being when General Obasanjo was elected as a civilian president on May 29, 1999.

General Obasanjo spent eight years as civilian president of Nigeria, with Abubakar Atiku as his vice president, and they handed over the office to Umaru YarAdua, with Dr Goodluck Jonathan as his vice president. Goodluck took over when Umaru died and was again re-elected for another term.

At the end of that term, he was not able to secure re-election, as General Muhammadu Buhari won the election and became a civilian president on 29 May 2015.

The minority people of Nigeria, including the Ogonis, Tivs, Benin, and Kalabari, just to mention a few among the about 450 tribes, were independent nations, and in their respective nations, they were not minorities. It is not that the minorities and the majorities are homogeneous groups and are exclusive as a concept. The minority/majority concept, however, is universal. And so, in every society, no matter how small or big that society is, minorities exist. With the colonialist intervention, our various nations accepted being subsumed under this larger nation called Nigeria. However, each group retained its pride, culture, common religion, and aspirations. The era when one group imposed on others its ideas, culture, religion, and so is outdated. In modern societies (with collective governance systems and with a guiding constitution), that is no longer possible.

We want, as a minimum standard, a political structure that will allow people to express some of their individualism as different people. Let the northern people practice sharia if they so wish within their regions. Let there be competition between the regions, as was the case in the first republic, so that these regions will be able to generate more revenue than the subventions they get. If these regions are put in place, some level of homogeneity will be achieved, and presidential elections will no longer generate this high level of tension and do-or-die mentality. Let us understand this: It is when we are proactive that we can achieve more and have peaceful coexistence and rapid national advancement.

Conclusion

Nigeria was a progressive federal state with three federating units immediately after independence. It became a unitary state after the military coup of 1966.

All the subsequently facilitated constitutions by the military ensured that it remained a unitary state with a false federalism to date. And the constitutions so made ensured that it would be difficult for the peoples of Nigeria to change the provisions of these constitutions.

Today, many people in Nigeria have realized that the nation will grow faster and become more peaceful if the peoples of Nigeria are allowed to stay together, in a union where each group can enjoy, unhindered, its uniqueness, culture, religion, aspirations, and healthy rivalry/peer cooperation among the federating units. Such would allow the federating units to decide for themselves how to develop their people on their own and contribute funds and other resources towards provision of agreed essential and necessary services by the central federal government. However, despite the obvious need for such a change, transforming Nigeria's governance into a democratic true federalism, as it once was, is becoming most impossible due to one major block—the emotions of some of us who prefer this exploitative intervention that encourages dependency by the falsely federating units (states).

We cannot chase shadows when the substantive target is visible and achievable. There is no gain without pain. Let every tribe and every state in Nigeria agree to make the sacrifice that is initially needed to see the nation through to an era of peace, tranquillity, friendship, and great progress.

3

Some Perspectives on the Evolution of Political System in Nigeria

The human is said to be political animal, and people have had the innate need from time immemorial to control their environment (which includes other human beings). Human beings over the years have continually improved their governance systems to suit the level of sophistication and political requirements of that time. Society requires leadership, and leadership functions well when there are constitutions—rules and regulations. It is the duty of leadership to enforce these rules and regulations. As society evolves, it gives greater governance participation to members of the society. So civilization will mean a more democratic system than one characterized by dictatorial leadership. Civilization is thus associated with the adoption of modes of governance that lean more toward persuasion and consultation than to confrontation.

I would use some form of classification of our political evolution to show how we have made progress (or lack thereof) in our governance system from earliest times. The system of classification I will propose may be somewhat arbitrary because, in reality, there are no clear-cut distinctions or boundaries between the stages I sketch out. What we see in reality is interplay of a mixed bag of systems, and at any time, a society would be classified by the most dominant system at play. I have, therefore, developed a paradigm of the development of political system including eight stages for the discussion, with jungle politics as the most primitive and politics of service as the most advanced.

I will now try to explain these evolutionary steps, elaborating on some of their attributes by using examples in our society.

3.1 Jungle Politics

This is the most primitive political evolutionary step. Early human beings were not living in well-organized societies, but their territorial defence and expansionist instincts were second to none, as these defined their need for survival.

The leaders in primitive societies were usually ruthless, and enforcement of established laws, especially those that would preserve the leader as long as he was alive, were taken seriously. For them, rebels must be deterred with maximum punishment, and killing of nonconformists or those who challenged the leader was normal.

Open criticism was usually considered a rebellious act; opposition could be considered a treasonable offence punishable by death.

It was a world of survival of the most powerful, and criterion for leadership was possession of fighting power and not necessarily any superiority of the intellect. Those who were strong warriors and who could protect the territory automatically became leaders.

It is usual for warriors who are leaders to desire annexing other territories they consider juicy. Intersocietal wars are frequent, and people born free today, if they are not killed by captors, become slaves tomorrow.

3.2 Religious Politics

Humankind is also said to be a religious animal. Most human beings are in one form of divine relationship or the other. Often, as new information became available, human beings who were not extremely conservative tended to modify some aspects of their religious beliefs in line with such new developments.

Societies evolved from jungle politics to religious politics because leaders realized it was easier to control their subjects on a sustainable basis with religious manipulations than with brute force. The religious leaders, who were often also part of the political leadership, ensured that everyone complied with rules and regulations that were set down. Stringent laws were also in place to ensure that no one disobeyed leadership. This has been the process that is applied from the traditional religious system to the foreign religions that came to us later. However, the introduction of foreign religions also changed the strategy to being more persuasive than confrontational. Often, there is a fine line between persuasion and manipulation. In all religious political systems, only ardent followers are rewarded with key political positions. This is often what happens when leaders give greater share of appointments to people who belong to their religion, cult, or secret society.

Intolerance is at its height in any society with a predominantly religious political system. The cause that Boko Haram is championing, the mindless killing of people of other faiths in certain areas of Nigeria in the name of mob riots from time to time, and the herdsmen killing spree are clear examples of the impacts of religious politics.

3.3 Ethnic Politics

Ethnic politics, like religion, encourages association of people with similarities and the suspicion or avoidance of people from different religions or ethnic groups. After our national independence, religion and ethnicity played a large role in Nigeria's emerging political systems. People often played the religious and ethnic cards to get support from their people. Children were indoctrinated, and there was much intolerance, prejudice, distrust, and hatred among the various ethnic groups.

These situations serve as fertile grounds for continuous ethno-religious conflicts that, if not properly managed, could eventually become the nemesis of the nation. People hate other people and do harmful things without considering the consequences of their actions. The problem is that conflicts have a tendency to spiral out of control when you least expect them, and bad people often hide behind mob actions to commit atrocities that can cause crisis.

Desperate politicians, who are losing relevance, resort to the ethnic card to retain or get followers.

Ethnic strife and violence will continue until we end ethno-religious politics.

3.4 Power Politics

Power politics is a refined form of jungle politics. The basis of emergence of leadership is power—the leader is the most powerful and has the ability to punish any non-conforming subject in society. There are different sources of power. In military regimes and at war times, guns are the source of power, and those who have them and can shoot with them are considered most powerful. At other times, money or political office may be the source of power. Everyone knows that anyone who rebels against a powerful leader will be punished. Assassinations, victimization, imprisonments, sack from employment, and lack of patronage, among other threats or punishments, are instruments used to put people in line.

These same sources of power can also be used to rig elections and ensure that popular mandates are stolen.

The Bible says that 'love of money is the root of all evil' and those who have a lot of money also have the power to get what they want. This means that any politician who wants to induce others to do what he or she wants in the future has to embezzle a lot of it now. For such politicians, therefore, corruption is a necessity.

The society is also at fault too. Due to moral poverty, societies tend to support and protect their corrupt sons and daughters. In fact, people tend to only criticize government officials who are not from their ethnic groups.

Many societies would consider a political officer foolish if he did not steal from the national wealth in his possession to benefit his people when he had the opportunity. Many societies idolize past politicians who unfairly used the common wealth to the exclusive benefits of their ethnic group members—be such benefit in the form of scholarship awards, empowerment programmes, appointments, or allocation of government developmental projects.

3.5 Democracy

The society that has evolved into democracy may still have elements of the other political systems still at play. Democracy means that the society recognizes the importance of majority decision-making. That means that people who have the advantage of religious or ethnic support would obviously want to use it to achieve majority support. A society that believes itself to be practicing democracy would be deceiving itself if it allows election rigging. This is because, often, in a rigged system, it is not the person who won the majority vote that would be declared winner. Such will be pseudo-democracy, as what that society is practicing is actually not democracy but any of the other primitive systems earlier discussed—namely, jungle, religious, ethnic, and power politics. In the absence of better systems, however, democracy is the most advanced political system. The other three systems yet to be discussed need democracy as a platform to operate.

Democracy, however, has its down sides too. Democracy encourages mediocrity, as majority decisions are usually not of the same quality compared to decisions taken by experts in the relevant fields. This deficiency becomes more prominent if the issue being decided on is highly technical. The outcome of majority decisions, however, can be improved if the electorate is educated through sensitization and debates before decisions are taken. How else can the electorate, who are mainly uneducated rural dwellers, decide on the best health strategy, the best way to generate jobs, the best political system the nation should adopt, and the best economic system for adoption, among other issues?

Decision-making should, therefore, be a two-pronged approach, where the populace explains what the issues are, what their problems are, and possible solutions so that this information becomes the raw materials that the experts will use to formulate appropriate solutions. Suggested solutions should again be taken to the masses for buy-in. I would say, therefore, that the best cut in any situation is to do an assigned job very well and not try to save costs by adopting untested shortcuts, which eventually will require a lot of rework.

The fact is that everybody is a minority in one form or the other. It is rare to find an individual who has not suffered discrimination as a minority in one area of life or the other. On the upside, however, democracy encourages broad-based participatory governance in a sense. It is not unusual for the majority to become monstrous and autocratic, which over a prolonged period disposes the minority to rebellious tendencies.

It is jungle democracy if a greedy majority uses its political power to confiscate the resources belonging to a minority group. Such is the case when oil-producing communities do not get developed as a result of resources found in their land because the decision as to how revenue will be allocated is made by the majority groups.

3.6 Politics of Inclusiveness

Based on the weaknesses in democracy, most democratic societies have evolved new democratic modifications that address the complaints of minorities. These include rotational systems, affirmative action, federal character, and so on. I do believe that these modifications equally to democracy may encourage mediocrity in some way, but giving every sector in a society some opportunity and some sense of belonging is a superior idea any day. For example, the system that encourages all political parties to share political appointments using religious or regional lines is great. Every section of this nation can govern itself if it is a nation of its own, and so there is no justification for any other group to arrogate to itself the decision of who is not competent to rule.

(I might be contradicting myself somehow here, but please bear with me, as life is full of contradictions.)

3.7 Politics of Ideas

Up till this point in this presentation, the main basis of political leadership selection or succession is on factors that have nothing much to do with leadership capacity, ability, expertise, and the like. The six systems so far discussed are driven by leadership selection that is mainly influenced by how powerful and warrior-like or how much money a potential leader has. It is also based on a potential leader's place of origin and connections.

This new system at least encourages selection of politicians who are knowledgeable about some of the issues and have some level of intelligence.

As society evolves and the younger generations begin to shed the ethno-religious baggage, where a politician comes from and his faith will become less and less important. What people will want to know is how competent the person is and the level of his or her integrity and willingness to serve unconditionally.

At that point, what matters is whether or not a leader will take a society to the next level. It will not matter if said leader is someone from a minority group, an atheist, or a woman.

Intellectual debates become a major basis of selecting the next set of leaders. Another advantage of debate is that it throws up new ideas from all sources (even from the opposition), which will be useful to whoever eventually becomes the leader.

3.8 Politics of Service

The seventh system of politics of ideas talks about competence, and competence does not necessarily translate to good performance. Competent leaders may not perform as a result of encumbrances, like the godfather factor, corruption, and so on. Politics of service goes further—from having ideas to performing well. Leaders who do not perform are voted out subsequently. Any society that is not able to remove any leader that has performed poorly due to many of the factors in the prior systems is not yet developed to the level of politics of service. Leaders of advanced societies who perform below expectation are easily removed, and we must make advancement towards being able to do that with ease. That way, people in authority will make sure they perform well to maintain their positions. This means, too, that leaders in every sector and at all levels should understand that they have to perform or leave office.

Societies that have evolved a service political system benefit greatly, as corruption is well managed, resources effectively applied, and goals and objectives are almost always achieved.

When a nation like Nigeria evolves a service politics system, then the legislators will have a conscience and will be guided by justice and fair play. In such a situation, the legislators will not allocate to themselves unfair portions of the national revenue.

In such systems, too, resources and revenue derived from minorities will be shared in a way that the people who own them will have a fair share of what they contribute to the national treasury. Doing otherwise will mean clear day robbery of defenceless people.

When service politics becomes the way of life, selfless service will be the aspiration of almost all politicians, and those who refuse will be voted out by the electorate.

3.9 Conclusion

At this point, the reader might be tempted to ask, what level of evolution is Nigerian politics at? The truth is shameful; it is a mixed bag of all the eight systems interplaying. This is because our institutions are not evolving and applying any effective rule of law. Impunity is now the order of the day and wearing a pair of trousers and roaming our streets freely. We disrespect people in authority for no just reason but respect only those who carry weapons and can shoot guns. The younger generations are being indoctrinated to believe that the end always justifies the means. If this continues, the youths who will be the leaders tomorrow will be worse than the people who have led us since independence. Many people no longer want to work to earn money. A number of people believe that the easiest way to become rich is to join the cult, steal crude oil, carry guns, rig elections, and so on and so forth. They see others go that way and get away with it, and so more are willing to take risks.

Is there a way forward? Yes, but it is mainly a mental reorientation thing, and our best bet is to concentrate on bringing up our children to be patriotic and good citizens. If that happens, intolerance and corruption will be seen by the society as bad when our children take over leadership.

For example, let us develop a process whereby incompetent judges who give judgments that are clearly below expectation are asked to go. As Nigerians, we should decide whether we want a part-time parliamentary system or this costly federal system. And we should decide whether to have a three-tier system of the federal government (FG), regions, and states; a four-tier system of federal government, regions, states, and LGAs; or to maintain the status quo. We need to give less funding and power to the federal government and give more to the lower tiers of government.

Let us talk about how to reduce ethnic and religious hatred and the Boko Haram menace.

I know the future is bright for our dear nation.

4

Some Key Issues to Be Handled to Improve Societal Advancement

4.1 Zoning and Federal Character Principles

I am in support of 'federal character' principle (FCP), as long as selections within the zones are done with merit.

We must place minimum standards for every selection process so that we do not place square pegs in round holes and glorify mediocrity and poor performance to high heavens.

For example, a minimum pass score should be given for entrance into Federal Unity Schools. The situation where students with scores less than 5 are in the same class with those that scored above 160 is counterproductive. Such people should either have a remedial arrangement to first prepare them or forfeit their chances to other sister states or people within the same catchment area until they have suitable candidates.

That same principle should apply in other areas where FCP needs to be applied. We must not just hand-pick people in each catchment area. Rather, we should always apply competitive meritocracy as the rule to throw up good candidates.

In view of the fact that we are many nations in one nation, we cannot wish away the federal character principle (FCP). The FCP ensures that every section of Nigeria has a sense of belonging.

This is a way of applying equity and not necessarily equality to address the fact that, if each section is a nation of its own, each will benefit from these services. So if we deprive them totally because they are less qualified than the other sections of the nation, then they are alienated, and they will be aggrieved over time.

What is expected from government and those applying FCP is to ensure that selection within the zones is made on merit.

We must accept that FCP cannot be applied in certain aspects of our national life:

- It is not applicable in the selection of a contingent to represent Nigeria in a competitive enterprise with other nations, be it sports, academics, or any other endeavour.
- It is not applicable in the selection of consultants or experts to handle sensitive national enterprises, including research or consultancy requiring the use of the best available brains.
- It should not be used in the selection of people to man the Central Bank, the minister in charge of finance, and any other appointment critical to the survival of the nation. Let the best available be appointed to these positions, and then the rest can be handled using the FCP.

It is, however, an important instrument for balancing political appointments. The following three aspects are proposed for consideration when FCP is to be applied:

1. ethnicity/state/north-south representation,
2. gender, and
3. religion.

My proposal, therefore, is that, whenever a political party takes a man as the presidential or gubernatorial candidate, the running mate should be a woman from a different religion and ethnic group. Similarly, if the candidate is a woman, then the running mate has to be a man from a different religion and ethnic group.

However, in the case of state or local government area appointments, where most people are of the same religion, then religion will not be a factor for consideration.

Such a system will make federal character more meaningful and more impactful. Since women account for 50 per cent of the population of Nigeria, it becomes injustice if a federal cabinet is made up of 90 per cent of males with very few women in it.

4.2 Enforcing Rules of Law and Reducing Impunity

- Impunity is impunity, but leadership impunity is the greatest travesty of democracy.
- It is dangerous for any nation to have political leaders, especially the president, the national assembly members, and the state governors, who arrogate to themselves powers beyond what is given to them by the constitution. They have ways of getting all the instruments of power to do their will.
- Crimes cannot be totally eliminated. However, if people know that, if they commit crimes, they will be investigated and the chances are high that they will be caught and prosecuted and that no one will be able to circumvent the law, as the guilty will be punished, then most people will be discouraged to commit crimes.
- It is a culture of lawlessness that makes people do whatever they like without any fear of retribution.

Every human has an instinct for survival, self-preservation, and consideration of self before others.

Those who have matured have extended this disposition to cover not only their individual selfish needs but also the collective needs of the larger society.

All resources and all assets belong to either an individual or a group of people. When an individual tries to corner the commonwealth for his or her sole use and benefit then that person is greedy. When that individual is able to do so brazenly and openly, without any reprimand, then that is impunity in display.

If what belongs to a nation is used to benefit only a section of the nation, what we are seeing is obviously greed, misappropriation, nepotism, corruption, and many other such negative and selfish misuses of public resources. Those who are victimized will feel unhappy and agitate for justice and equity.

The same applies in the states of the federation, and the same applies in our various local governments. The same applies also in our respective communities, homes, and families.

There is a pervasive culture of corruption and impunity in all spheres of our lives, not because we are really bad people but because everyone knows that those in authority can do anything and get away scot-free.

Based on this atmosphere of impunity, those who have no business in politics have hijacked it because it is the real goldmine in Africa. Many who become governor, president, minister, senator, and federal or state legislator are rich for life. Some of them will always devise means of stealing and hiding their loot. Is it every politician that is bad then?

To answer that question, I will ask another rhetorical one: How can a clean finger coexist with oily fingers? Will any Nigerian politician agree to stay clean when that person has spent his or her life savings and those of his or her sponsors to get elected? Most people in politics are driven by the desire to become rich; there is no very clean person in the political arena.

Now, the question is, must this situation remain the same, or can we, as the people who suffer the brunt of the current system, do something to end it and put in place a new system? Yes, and that is what the developed nations have done. They have made corruption so unattractive that many will not want to venture into it. Now, how can you change a thing when those who are to change it are the ones benefiting from it? Many politicians I know would like to abandon the current situation if they knew that the effort to make Nigeria better would succeed. I do not advocate for violent revolution. However, if nothing is done, then it is inevitable that the situation will continue to deteriorate until it culminates in a spontaneous violent reaction. And that is what we do not want.

We want to reorient the new generation that will take over from this crop of politicians who are too far gone in this greedy lifestyle. They simply take from the commonwealth—with abandon and utter insensitivity—money they do not need. One man or woman will desire to take everything if he or she can, so that every other Nigerian will be his or her slave.

Such a practice is madness, but it is so common that this abnormality no longer appears abnormal. It is now the tradition and way of life of many people. A righteous politician who refuses to enrich himself while in office will probably be ostracized by his community when he comes back home empty-handed.

If all nations have passed through this phase in their national developmental history, then we too can outgrow it.

The only problem is that, if nothing is done, we might stay in this barbaric and primitive phase for eternity.

Have you asked yourself how you can contribute as an individual towards our rapid national development? Are you satisfied with our backwards and retrogressive development when others, even some African nations, are making good progress?

How have you helped in your small way in your office to discourage this scourge? How can our universities contribute? How can our community heads all contribute? Our churches and our religious leaders, are they showing a good example? Don't say you are insignificant. Little drops of water can make a mighty ocean.

Come, let us reason together in unity and make progress. Though we are all sinners, though all of us have been involved in one act of corruption or the other and though those who have not been in power are hoping that, one day, their turn will come to steal, we need to make amends for the sake of our fatherland, our only real home, the place we shall bequeath to our future generations. We must leave for our children's children a nation that all other nations will want to emulate—a nation every black man will call the pride of his race.

Impunity has been practiced with total abandon with regards to allocation of resources to the governed. The constitution has stipulated that the commonwealth should be shared justifiably and equitably among all the peoples of the nation and appointments should be made in line with the federal character. No matter the weaknesses of these federal character provisions, they have been made with good intentions to avoid possible abuse by political leaders with primordial tendencies. However, these provisions are still circumvented and usually encouraged by 'his or her people'—people from the leader's ethnic group with their agenda propelled by greed.

It is, therefore, normal for the president or governors to arrogate to themselves power to allocate developmental projects to ethnic groups or state and local governments without recourse to anyone. A president will openly say a group will not be given any projects because they did not vote for him. Though it is wrong to discriminate for any reason, it is double irony if the revenue to be shared came mainly from the ethnic group that is so punished for not voting for the president. In decent societies, the revenue sharing should favour those from where said revenue was derived.

The problem with our democratic leaders is that they still think they have the powers of our primitive traditional kings of the past. They still think their pronouncements cannot be questioned. They see every criticism as challenge of their authority and so something that must be controlled.

Though most of what I will say below is not new and has been mentioned by many in different fora, I would like to reiterate the following as suggestion to be considered in addressing the above problem:

- Nigeria should consider recognizing the six geopolitical regions or zones of North East, North West, North Central, South West, South East, and South South as the federating units.
- These regions should form their own governments, with only one legislative body made up of five persons from each of the constituent states. The National Assembly should

27

also be made up of one body, the Senate having only three persons representatives from each state and with no House of Representatives.

- Each region will have a maximum of ten ministries, including finance, sustainable development, electricity, infrastructure, culture and tourism, health, and education.
- These six regions will independently develop their natural resources and export same to generate income in any form, be it raw or refined.
- The six regions will have the powers to engage experts or partners to help them develop their respective regions without hindrances from anyone.
- Though the federal government can establish cross-cutting infrastructural projects to benefit more than one region—for example, rail lines, power-generating plants, major highways, and the like—it is the duty of the respective regions to run efficient rail systems using trains in collaboration with experts or partners. Every region must have more than one service provider to eliminate monopoly and ensure competitive efficiency. Government must provide the infrastructure, including things like standard gauge rail tracts, hydro dams, and so forth. These will be rented to service providers, who will provide the trains, as in the case of a rail system, and run them efficiently.
- Alongside these regional governments, state governments will run independent of them. The state governments can also have their own ministries aligned to the regional arrangement, but all elections for offices at the regions or states will be handled by the Independent National Electoral Commission.
- Revenue sharing will be 50 per cent going to the state in the region from where it is derived, 30 per cent going to the region, and 20 per cent going to the federal government. Other revenue directly derived by the region will still be shared 50 per cent to be shared by all the states in the region, 30 per cent to be retained by the region and 20 per cent given to the federal government.

- Each region can choose to have a state religion if at least 70 per cent of its population belongs to one religion. However, even in regions where a state religion exists, every individual will still exercise his or her freedom of choice of religion and association and will be free to practice it without any molestation whatsoever.

Considering the fact that these over-imposing and greedy political leaders exist at all levels—in the federal government, regional government, state levels and even at the local government—it is important that we begin to build institutions strong enough to resist manipulation by any of the arms of government. We should set up a national monitoring body, whose duty will be to ensure that the various governments are ensuring equitable distribution of revenue, funds, resources, amenities, and appointments. This new body will not report to the president. The appointment will be made by the Senate, and officers so appointed can only be removed by a 75 per cent Senate affirmation. The president can nominate ten persons, and the Senate will vote and pick only one person for the appointment. Apart from the chairman appointed by the Senate, each state will have a member appointed by the state's house of assembly, who is similarly appointed and who can also be removed only by that state assembly with 75 per cent affirmation.

Where any political officer at the federal, regional, or state level is found to have defaulted, that person will be taken to the courts. Such person can be removed by the court and not necessarily by the Senate. Immunity of political office holders shall not apply here. These ideas are proposed to control the continuous abuse of power by holders of political offices in Nigeria.

If we have righteous leaders, who make the nation grow, we begin deteriorating when they leave office and bad leaders take over. If, however, we develop our institutions to function effectively, the institutions will not allow bad leaders to take us backwards. We should put in place enduring structures that will prevent corruption, discrimination, victimization, and encourage transparency and meritocracy.

We want transformation that will be embedded in our consciousness, especially among our children who will be the future leaders, so that we instinctively know in our collective consciousness what is good from what is bad.

Now, what role will the local governments have in all this, since they are the ones at the grassroots?

- Local governments (LGs) should be politically, financially, administratively, and legislatively free from the state government. They should be an independent arm of government and should get their subventions directly from the source. There is nothing wrong with having four tiers of government, so long as they are well ran.

- No state government should be allowed to appoint caretakers for local governments. Neither should a state government have the power to sack the chairman of a local government. LG chairmen can only be impeached by the local government's legislative bodies.

- LG elections should be handled by INEC and not state bodies, who may be more motivated to rig the elections.

- All stand-alone developmental projects should be implemented by the LGs. The LGs are closer to the grassroots and in a better position to know what the people need.

- Only projects that are cross-cutting and will benefit more than one city in a state should be handled by the state government. Examples include roads that link cities within the state, schools, and hospital administration. Such projects can be handled by the state government. The remainder and bulk of projects should by handled by the LG. It follows that the revenue sharing formula needs to be reviewed again in line with this system.

It also follows that LGs will have great responsibilities and so should be better audited annually. EFCC should have functional offices in every LG area in Nigeria. The EFCC should give annual performance appraisals to the Senate and the president.

There is abuse of office at every level, but no one has the right to use the commonwealth to satisfy only selfish interests.

On the other hand, the position of the 2014 National Conference is that local governments should become administrative units of their respective states. That means that no specific allocation would be made to them, as they would be subsumed under their state government's accruable revenue. This arrangement would have been ideal, as it would have addressed the lopsided allocation to local governments by the military facilitated constitution favouring the northern states. However, to adopt this system, we would also need to put in place a process to ensure that state governments gave equal attention to all local governments and were not able to implement projects using parochial considerations.

In social science, there is rarely a single silver bullet that can address every problem. And when you seek sustainable advancement, you seek a consensus opinion born out of the myriad of opinions from all groups in a nation. I wish to again propose another revised version:

- *Win-win* means listening to each other, not shouting your opinions down the throats of others and insisting on your view without considering the opinions of others.
- Restructuring in the long run will favour everybody.
- Restructuring is better than the demand for secession because, if war starts again, for whatever reason, then Nigeria is likely not going to remain the same. That will be very disadvantageous to all, including the north.
- Devolve more power to the states or regions, make local governments administrative units to reduce the disparity and because most states are not viable. I propose two options: One, we should collapse the states into six or twelve states so that the current states serve the LGAs' intended purpose. Or, two, we should leave the thirty-six states, plus one more for the south-east, as the only federating units without a larger regional arrangement, in which case, each state will be forced on its own to cut its clothes according to its lot.

- For both options, allow independent regions and/or states to generate revenue and pay tax to the federal government. Don't be afraid that some regions will suffer. That won't actually be the case, as the tax collected for sharing by all can, to some extent, be high enough to cushion the shortfall from internally generated revenue.

- For option one, 40 per cent of revenue generated by each region should be given to the federal government, who will retain 20 per cent and share the balance 20 per cent equitably to all the regions. The region retains 60 per cent of what is generated, using 20 per cent for regional services and sharing 10 per cent equitably to the states within the region. The remaining 30 per cent of the revenue is retained by the state where it was generated.

- For option two, 50 per cent is retained by the state where it is generated and the remaining 50 per cent is given to the federal government. The federal share is again shared—20 per cent retained for national projects and 30 per cent shared among the states equitably.

- We must also remember to make governance less expensive. Reduce the legislative members numerically, and reduce their remunerations.

- There must be a statuary provision that any president or governor who does not equitably (not equally) allocate projects and appointments within his or her area of governance, in line with the federal character principle, should be removed by either the relevant legislative house or the courts.

- Another important point to note is that 13 per cent derivation will no longer be applicable. Instead 30 per cent of whatever accrues to the state in option one or two will be shared equally by the generating LGA and the generating communities.

Let us restructure now and practice the true federalism we profess.

4.3 Curbing Revenue Generation Indolence in Governance

Indolence is common with regards to revenue generation by the various arms of government in Nigeria, since money comes in every month for sharing. Though all the state governments always talk about renewed efforts to increase their revenue bases, it is mostly lip service. Year in year out, the situation remains the same, except in a few hardworking states.

More than 50 per cent of the states in Nigeria bring in more or less nothing to the federal coffers for sharing. The constitution, tailored by the former military government, has made sure of that. Rather, it is the very states that bring in nothing by way of revenue that threaten the nation with wars if anyone tries to change the existing sharing formula or political situation.

Many of the states are, therefore, not viable. Rather than seeking solutions, many more states are agitating further division so that they can attract more subventions from the federal government.

My worry is about the unsustainable nature of this arrangement and the dependency mentality associated with it. Just imagine what will happen if the value of crude oil becomes more or less worthless with time, as was the case with coal. Imagine what will happen in less than fifty years from now when most of our crude oil-producing fields will have dried up. The truth is that a number of them have already dried up or are about to. Just imagine what will become of Nigeria, our exorbitant and unreserved project budgeting, our lifestyle of wastefulness and profligacy. Just imagine what will happen to the people and the economy.

While most nations budget in ways that include savings and investments, we not only budget everything annually, but we also spend more than we can generate. Therefore, we are always in deficit.

We are accumulating debts for our future generations to pay. And their capacity to pay will be highly limited if we use the funds to implement non-productive ventures like paying allowances to our lawmakers or giving handouts to unemployed youths who we hope will vote for our party in the future.

The 2014 National Conference by Nigeria, facilitated by Dr Goodluck Jonathan, then president, attempted to address many national issues, including form and structures of government, devolution of powers, revenue sharing, resource control, state creation, state police, and fiscal federalism, among others. However, in this section, I wish to mention two potential solutions for reducing this dependency mentality, in which our federating units are dependent on subvention: The first is a restructuring of the national federating units to be more able and more motivated to generate revenue for themselves and the central government invariably. The second involves using the restructured federating units to become more interested in the exploration, exploitation, and production of more mineral resources to generate revenue. That conference, as reported by Professor Godini G. Darah, was the seventeenth to be held in Nigeria since the 1914 amalgamation.

Professor Darah went on to explain that the 2014 National Conference obtained from the Ministry of Solid Minerals Development the list of forty-two commercially viable solid minerals in Nigeria. He stated that the states of Taraba and Plateau alone each has about twenty-five such minerals and that some of them exist in quantities greater than what is available in some continents.

The report also said that the bitumen deposit discovered since 1913—for example, in Ondo, Edo, and Lagos—states discovered since 1913—is second in volume to that of Venezuela, South America. However, rather than produce, use, and export this resource, Nigeria has been importing bitumen for its road construction. In the same way, we export crude oil for pittance and import refined products with our hard-earned foreign exchange. Similarly, we have been flaring gas and burning potential revenue and highly valued natural resources since we started producing crude oil as far back as 1959 to date.

We must change our current mentality and begin adopting sustainable approaches to governance. Nigeria cannot be parasitic; we must learn to be of value to other nations. We must develop products that will be useful to our neighbouring nations and others far and wide.

We must add value to our raw materials before we export them so that we get more money from them. Nigeria depending on developed nations for aids is parasitic, and states doing nothing but depending on revenue from other states for their own sustenance is equally parasitic.

The majority of Nigerians have only Nigeria as their only home. Those with dual citizenships equally love Nigeria deeply.

We all, therefore, have a stake in ensuring that we do not, in the future, become one of the poorest nations in the world, despite the God-given opportunity we have had to use our endowments to become one of the most developed nations in the world.

I know that most of the states in Nigeria will not be able to stand on their own in the near future if the windfall income we get from sales of crude oil dwindles. This is obvious since even with these incomes, most states cannot pay salaries to their workers. It is so pathetic.

I cannot understand why these governments cannot be frugal and cut their clothes according to their lots.

Everyone can agree with me that the governance system we are using now is not sustainable. It is only a fool who will see a debilitating crisis in the future and still move head-on into it.

Our sentiments may urge us on, but we need to re-examine our strategic plans now while we still have some leeway.

Since most of these states are just waste pipes, frittering away our revenues, we have no other viable option but to think strategically and develop a new sustainable governance system that will not only allow us to grow today but also enable us to remain sustainable and competitive when our current sources of revenue become less productive.

Among other things, we must collapse the many states into a few viable ones so that they can all become productive, with lower overhead costs, independence, and the ability to generate enough revenue to take care of their recurrent costs. That way, any additional revenue that comes to them from subventions or savings from incomes or royalties will be used to further develop critical aspects of the economy and move Nigeria boldly and proudly into the class of developed nations of the world as a nation of all black people.

4.4 Empowerment of Women as Tool for National Development

In the year 2017, many traditions still discriminate against the girl child. What is the reason a daughter cannot share in her parents' inheritance? Why should a married woman be considered sold-out chattel that cannot make claims to her parents' inheritance?

The irony is that we are the same people who encourage our relatives whose mothers are from places like the United Kingdom and the United States to apply for dual citizenship. Let it be clear that the woman is as human as the man and should have the same rights.

Why can't the children of our daughters share in benefits accruing to their mothers' place of birth? Why should a woman be deprived of her husband's property when he dies?

Someone told me that it is constitutional that you claim only your father's place of origin and not that of your mother. I did not see that in the Nigerian Constitution, and if it were so written, it would elevate discrimination against women to a deplorable height.

Women constitute about 50 per cent of the population of Nigeria. So, if we are about 180 million people, then we have about 90 million Nigerian women. This population of women is greater than the entire population of most countries in Africa. It is a phenomenal 'depot of resources' that can transform our nation into a powerful internationally recognizable force.

In most Nigerian societies women are relegated to the background. They are not consulted in community affairs, even when the issue directly affects them. I have visited many communities in Nigeria where I held meetings with the community members. Things are changing gradually, but unless you specifically ask for the attendance of women, you may not see a single woman at the gathering.

At the family front, women contribute greatly to the upkeep of the home and upbringing of the children. Let us remind ourselves by listing a few of the important roles women traditionally play in society:

- Women also work hard to raise money to either fend or subsidize what their husbands bring in.
- Women are actively involved in most livelihood businesses.
- Women farm, fish, and trade to raise money.

To a degree, things are changing now, and more girls are allowed to acquire a Western education. That is still not the case, however, in remote conservative societies within the nation.

Nevertheless, experience has shown that girls perform as well or even better than their male counterparts academically. They equally perform as well or even better as workers in organizations. There are no longer careers or professions dedicated to only men or women.

Despite what has been said above, most parents would prefer to educate or train their male children if they have to choose as a result of inadequate funds for all.

Our cultures have been conservative, and most traditions have not changed from time immemorial. If culture is dynamic, and if we ended the killing of twins, among others, as bad cultural practices now left in the past, then it is time our cultures gave the same respect to both sexes.

The girl child has the same rights as the boy child. The girl child should share in her parents' inheritance as a matter of right. The children of the women in our society should be able to choose to claim citizenship of either parent, since they are products of both parents. Marriage is not about selling the woman; it is simply a process and an institution to recognize the great and godly union of two individuals.

Every culture that sees the girl child as inferior to the boy child, unable to partake in inheritance, is as discriminatory and backward as a culture that permits slavery. The girl child is not a substandard entity to the boy child. We must, therefore, give our female children all the respect and all the opportunities we give our male children.

It was reported by Child Rights Awareness Creation Organization (CRACO) (www.cracong.org) in 2017 that the supreme court voided the Igbo law and custom that does not allow females to inherit their late fathers' estates, on the grounds that it is discriminatory and conflicts with the provision of the constitution.

The following are extracts from the report. It reads:
The court held that the practice conflicted with section 42(1)(a) and (2) of the 1999 Constitution.

It went on to say:

No matter the circumstances of the birth of a female child, such a child is entitled to an inheritance from her late father's estate. Consequently, the Igbo customary law, which disentitles a female child from partaking in the sharing of her deceased father's estate, is breach of Section 42(1) and (2) of the Constitution, a fundamental rights provision guaranteed to every Nigerian. The said discriminatory customary law is void as it conflicts with Section 42(1) and (2) of the Constitution

We must give equal voices to women in our family and community meetings. We must allow women to take decisions in affairs that concern them.

Some ethnic groups are already practicing this principle of equality, and I see those cultures that currently give the same rights to both sexes as more advanced in this respect. Those still behind need to catch up because God the Creator sees all humanity as equal in this respect. There is no human right provision that should consider the female child inferior in any respect to the male child.

Rights come with responsibilities. No woman should think that the management and upkeep of homes are not joint responsibilities of husband and wife. The principle should be equity, where partners contribute to the upkeep of homes according to their endowment and blessings.

Should women take leadership positions in the church in line with their gifts? Oh, yes! In modern times, we have come to understand that women are never and should not be seen as inferior human beings.

Nigerian womenfolk are performing significantly better than women from other African nations in many fields of endeavour. This trend is evident in endeavours like football, athletics, and other games; academics; entertainment; banking; engineering; politics and legal professions; medicine; religion; and so on.

Two possible explanations can be given for this: One is that our women are genetically very strong. The other is that previous cultural hindrances are being eliminated, and our female folks are now experiencing freedom with regards to decision-making as it affects their lives. Women are now being allowed to follow their career aspirations freely without too much opposition, even in sports, the military, entertainment, and other professions.

We are making progress. But we have not yet achieved the desired level of equality, as many cultural and religious hindrances still exist.

4.5 The Negative Impacts of Superstition and Ritualism

Nigeria is said to have about 450 ethnic groups, and we have equally as many religious gods as we have tribes. Most of these gods are creations of our traditional religion. To that extent, I would subscribe to the adage that we human beings created our gods in the likeness of our thinking. Ancestral religions and beliefs affect our approach to and way of life. They affect our cultures and tradition. Many Nigerians are religious, and most religions require that adherents do not question their veracity. Superstition is this unquestionable belief of magical powers that defy logic and science.

Are superstitious beliefs bad? I would rather not comment. However, illogical pursuit of dangerous, devilish, greedy, and criminal activities in the name of religion is bad. Someone has said that religion is the opium of the masses. I would think that religion has the power to calm the nerves of the poverty-stricken suffering masses; it has powers to relieve pains of hunger, drudgery, slavery, and other societal ills. To me, that aspect of religion is good. Religion reduces the level of crimes in society, as most religious beliefs discourage antisocial acts.

Those who are deeply superstitious are equally deeply fanatical. These attributes block their thinking abilities, as they make deliberate efforts to think narrowly, stipulating to the confines of their religion, beliefs, or myths. The implication is that people do not get superstitious only because of religious beliefs, but also because of a belief in various forms of magic, hearsay, charlatans, and the like. Whatever the source, such blind beliefs make them superstitious.

Many years ago, some people were killing twins and albinos, illustrating the depths to which people can sink in ignorance and superstition. Today, we still have many cultural practices that are equally barbaric and primitive, with superstitious justifications. Though many of such practices are now illegal, they still happen at times. Imagine that some people still believe that human body parts or killing and sacrificing human beings can attract favour from Satan and his agents. This is the reason we still have ritual killings in some places. How can this be further discouraged?

In the Nigeria of 2017, ritualistic killings are still common. For God's sake, there is no link between human body parts and mystic power. Nevertheless, many indulge in these practices, and in desperation, people still believe these things. Stop killing people because of idiotic superstition.

Even if it works through satanic manipulation, why are people so wicked and desperate?

The truth is that these practices do not work. If the devil is only using these means to deceive the gullible into spilling blood of innocent people and to keep fools in his perpetual bondage, why choose that slavery?

People can believe anything. Satan is exploiting that human capacity to the extent that desperate people are encouraged to kill fellow human beings wantonly.

Some persons believe that, if you kill a fellow being or sacrifice human body parts to dead gods or powerless evil spirits, they will be rewarded with success. If those evil spirits were so powerful, why would they need humans to kill for them? It does not make any sense and is, at best, primitive logic.

Are we still so uncivilized? Do we still practice human sacrifice in this age and time?

I pray that we shall improve our investigative skills so that all involved in these savage acts will be apprehended, prosecuted, and punished adequately.

A good number of Nigerians and Africans believe strongly in the potency of witchcraft, myths, superstition, metaphysical sacrifices, and ritualism for success.

Consider these questions: If you have done a ritual sacrifice for a competition, why are you not the champion of the nation in that field? Why do you still practice even harder than others who have not made ritual sacrifice so that you will win? Is it that you do not totally believe in the efficacy of ritualism?

4.6 Encouraging Education for All in Nigeria

Illiteracy is lack of the ability to read and write. It is a disability because, if you are illiterate, you are confined to only information relayed to you by others. You cannot, on your own, choose to quest for knowledge independently until you can read and write. If this disability is compounded with inability to speak a commonly spoken language or lingua franca, your ability to interact with people outside your immediate environment is highly impaired. In addition, illiteracy reduces your ability to personally manage your finances or carry out banking and other financial transactions.

Illiteracy is not the same thing as ignorance, though the two are related. Illiteracy can predispose one to some level of ignorance, and this can discourage a person from pursuing education. Illiteracy is equally a good fertile ground in which to encourage superstitious beliefs.

I would not categorize someone with an Islamic education only as an illiterate, but in modern-day Nigeria, people must have a 'balanced' education to enable them fit properly into the scheme of things and acquire relevant skills that can enable them further interact well with the world. For functional reasons, therefore, persons who are literate in Islamic education should do themselves a favour by taking on some aspects of Western education.

In the modern world, people are not expected to depend on others to explain written instructions and information, as everyone is expected to have a minimum level of education to be able to read and write the commonly used language of the nation.

The benefits of education and literacy are both individual and social. Educated persons are healthier persons. They tend to engage in more health-seeking behaviours. Educated women have fewer children and take better care of their kids. Educated persons manage their environments better and follow instructions better. The benefits of education are, thus, endless.

Anyone deprived of education has been deprived of his or her ability to attain his or her greatest potentials. Every person has gifts. Some are potentially the most gifted, for instance, medical doctors. And some are potentially the people that will develop inventions that would radically change the world for good in every field of pursuit, including medicine, engineering, law, politics, and technology in general. Depriving these young ones from acquiring education not only deprives them from becoming independent self-sustaining individuals pursuing their own career interests but also deprives the world from benefiting from the gifts and potentials they have.

Apart from these benefits of literacy and education, those with education are more likely not to be superstitious and more likely not to be menial workers. Similarly, they are more likely not to be influenced by desperate politicians to serve as political thugs or suicide bombers.

In the same way, government and churches should make every effort to educate adults who are still illiterate, to enable them to enjoy a better quality of life.

4.7 Lack of Balanced Education: The Almajiri System as a Culprit

The Almajiri caste system is the main culprit in the ever-increasing menace of homeless beggars as people procreate more children than they can carter for. These children are not given proper education or life-sustaining skills. As these Almajiri children grow into adulthood, they become social misfits and are easily used by people to commit crimes and terrorism.

It is, therefore, a laudable idea that those who are poor should not marry more women than they can care for. However, the implementation of this bill, made in Kano state in 2017 and supported by the respected Emir of Kano, may be resisted by traditionalists and conservatives. They will argue over the criteria used to assess poverty, despite the availability of the United Nation's standard of what constitutes poverty.

The bill should not only target poor people but should also encourage the wealthy to reduce the number of wives they take on. This is because today's economic situation may not guarantee that it will be same tomorrow. Those who are rich today and marry many wives and subsequently have many children may have difficulty if they become less wealthy in the future.

Nigeria's population is rapidly exploding, and this boom will overtake that of nations like the United States of America and a number of others in a few years because there is no effective family planning here. While developed wealthy nations are controlling their populations and are economically growing, in Nigeria, we are increasing our population while deteriorating economically.

Nigeria should equally teach family planning, sex education, and civic education to all its citizens in primary and secondary schools. Nigeria should make education compulsory and free for all Nigerian pupils in order to reduce illiteracy.

The Almajiri caste system on the surface does not look discriminatory, as no group seems to be targeted for discriminatory practices. However, it has all the attributes of a discriminatory caste system. As in most class-conscious societies, the children of the poor and orphans have fewer opportunities to achieve their potentials in life.

If these children do not have education and cannot acquire capacities to fend for themselves, then they will eventually die poor and at much younger ages than will their wealthier counterparts. This is obvious because they cannot raise the money that enables a good quality of life, and death is a likely consequence anytime they fall really sick. Their children, too, are exposed to early death and are more likely to be attracted to a life of crimes for sustenance and drug abuse for escape.

It is, therefore, a caste system. Those at poverty level will remain poor for life, no matter how they try, and so will their children's children.

Apart from that fact, those who belong to higher social class levels would not want to interact with them as equals. They use those in the lower classes to provide menial services in jobs like gateman, gardener, and so on as may be required as I advanced in the previous subsection. In addition, people from these lower classes are indoctrinated and are ready tools in the hands of wicked people, who use them as foot soldiers in committing social crimes like political and religious insurgencies.

Class-consciousness is a common thing in Nigeria, and people unconsciously are expected to marry, relate with, and be friends with people within the same class bracket as them.

In view of the above, government has a major role to play in ending this Almajiri caste system by providing free and incentive-packed education so that most of the poorer class will have the opportunity to grow out of this inhuman poverty in which they find themselves. It is their fundamental human right like all other Nigerian children to have at least a free basic education up to the junior secondary school class 3, by which time they will have acquired at least a technical skill as a source of livelihood.

4.8 Giving Proper and Relevant Education to Nigerians

Education builds capacities of individuals in terms of knowledge and experience and broadens their understanding of the environment, including people they must interact with. Education obviously helps in enhancing self-reliance, self-worth, and self-esteem. The most critical deliverable of education is to give the educated the skills to solve day-to-day problems and challenges. Education will be incomplete if it does not inculcate in the person, national consciousness, patriotism, and the ability for independent thinking.

Through education, useful cultural practices and other survival skills are transmitted from one generation to the other.

Education is also useful as a tool to liberate, transform, reorient, and heal the sick. If people are aware of the harm their actions cause to the environment, they may change their destructive activities.

It is for the above reasons that a more robust educational policy is being advocated for all Nigerians to cover children, youths, adults, communities, and the masses.

Education can be both formal and informal. Informal education starts from birth, with the major roles played by the parents and others involved in raising the child. Formal education is carried out by professionals involved in teaching at the various levels.

There has been an argument with regards to declining standard of education. Some say it is declining because pupils in the final year in primary school about fifty years ago could write and speak good English language while, these days, people who have finished secondary education may still not be able to write simple statements without making mistakes. The other aspect relates to the content of what is taught now as compared to what was taught several years ago. These days, pupils in primary schools learn a lot more subjects, ranging from science to civic education to computer science and a lot more, while in the past, only a few subjects were taught.

On the other hand, others argue that, while most public schools are poorly managed and so do not give a good education, a few schools, though mainly private schools, are well run and so still maintain high-quality education.

For education to be relevant, it has to prepare the students to become useful to society and to themselves. It is useless for young people to leave a secondary or tertiary institution without acquiring any skill that would enable them to stand on their own if they do not secure employment in the already oversaturated labour market.

The other issue of contention has been the inability of government to properly fund education. The inability has resulted in frequent industrial disputes between teachers or lecturers and government. Such disputes invariable affect the students more than the disputants.

Gradually, this need to provide qualitative education is being effectively taken over by the private sector. This has been completed in the primary and secondary school levels.

It has commenced at the tertiary levels, and soon private universities will be providing superior services to what is provided by the federal and state governments.

Additional reasons parents are moving their wards to private universities at this time have to do with the following:

1. Private universities provide assurance that students will graduate when due to do so because there is no frequent disruption of the academic calendar as a result of strikes. This is not to indict the universities but to say that the funding conflicts between government and the universities is affecting the students adversely both in terms number of years they stay in the university and in terms of the quality of education, when semesters are rushed in a way that a three-month semester is cramped into one and a half months and so on.
2. Some schools are becoming notorious for their many lecturers who expect gifts from students as a basis for getting good grades. This is what students call 'sorting.'
3. Some universities are notorious despite the effort made to rid our institutions of cultism.
4. The number of prospective students seeking admissions is overwhelming and cannot be handled by the government universities. Since the private universities are cheaper than sending wards abroad, parents have to make do with private ones so that their children will not only get admitted but also get the course of study that they desire.

Governments must fund universities properly to ensure standards are maintained. They must rank universities in terms of professions, for example the schools of medicines, faculties of law, business schools, faculties of engineering and so on each should be ranked separately. And the universities have to find ways to generate funds to run their programs effectively if they want to remain relevant in the future.

4.9 Role of Competition in Improving Standards

Competition is a very important aspect of life and nature. Charles Darwin called it survival of the fittest and we know that humankind started life with competition. One male sperm had to compete against several others in a race to fertilize the available egg in the female. To survive in the jungle, you must learn from more experienced people how to avoid predators and how to prey on others. Everyone in competition is desperate to win to have the respect and admiration of others, and those who witness the competition see it first as entertainment but subconsciously are also in competition, having taken sides with either opponent. Those who are victorious are elated and happy, while those who lost are sad and dejected. Competitions are made more intriguing and contestants more committed when there is a good prize for winning.

Contestants, therefore, devote much time to preparing for competition in order to win. Depending on the nature of the competition, relevant skills are acquired and perfected.

It can therefore be said that human beings are wired to see competition as something they must win. To humans, not winning in a competition is an erosion of their pride and self-worth. Often, winning comes with high-stake rewards, and so people put in all their efforts; some are ready to stake their own lives to win such competitions.

Humankind is so wired in a way that any competition is seen as a must win. We feel we must win even when it comes to competition for fun or competition in which we are not participating but for which we have taken a side.

Human beings have outshined all other animals in nature due to humanity's intellectual endowments. Our activities and need for expansion as we populate the earth threaten other organisms with extinction.

We equally compete among ourselves for scarce resources. These competitions are part of our ways of living.

In nature, competition is aimed at eliminating weak genes and allowing only adapted products to survive, and the same principle is utilized to select suitable candidates for any position. By subjecting candidates to a selection competition, one can identify and pick the best suitable for the position. The implication of this principle is that organizations that wish to perform well must choose the best candidates through a competitive selection process and not through nepotism, cronyism, and the like. Engagement of such less competent people is the first stage of the downfall of any organization.

Since competition mimics nature and sustains continuous improvement in all aspects of life, man has exploited this aspect of humanity as big business. We compete in sports (football, athletics, boxing, and wrestling to mention but a few). We compete in reality TV shows like *Big Brother Africa*, singing competitions, and on and on. We have many competitions, including beauty contests and even gambling events.

Just as we compete for fun, people in the business world compete for survival. The market is vast, but they are very selective. Good-quality product at highly reduced costs is required. Those who are innovative and churn out superior products attract customers and, in so doing, become rich. There is competition in every business enterprise, music, arts, book writing, comedy—just name it.

The good thing here is that competition brings about continuous improvement of the various products, and humanity is better for it.

How can we as a nation benefit from this competitive spirit in the formation of our national teams? I will use football as an example, but the principle can be applied in any competition.

The inter-primary schools football competitions being sponsored by Channels TV and organizations like them are good social corporate responsibility interventions. However, it is not an ideal platform for scouting because it has an inherent weakness, as some of the most talented players fall through the cracks when their teams are eliminated as the competition progresses.

Our proposal is that the competition ends at the community or local government area levels. The team to represent each LGA will not come from one school but from a composite, where the best of each position—goalkeeper, left and right wingers, midfielders, defenders, and so on—will be selected from the various schools. That way, the best players will constitute the team. Similarly, the team to represent the states in the interstate competition will be composite selection from the various LGAs in the state.

Though the proposal is more complex than the current structure, it is the best way to scout for a dream team with the very best talents for future members of the national team. A similar process is equally important for the secondary schools, where players so selected will be ready for national assignments in the nearest future.

The Federal Ministry of Sports should coordinate this as a matter of urgency. The ministry should engage all key companies and multinationals operating in Nigeria for collective sponsorship. It is time we revived first our football and then later other sports.

Competition is also a way to ensure people continue having interest in our cultural activities and to encourage tourism. We can encourage competition in cultural dances and masquerade displays; traditional foods; traditional games and sports, even traditional wresting; and on and on.

Competition also has negative implications. Wars and the cruelties of wars are part of the evils of competition. Rigging during elections, betting with money, gambling, cult rivalries, territorial aggressions, and the like have all ruined contestants and claimed lives.

In this area, there is also the wrong application whereby devious entrepreneurs create artificial scarcity of commodities so that prices of goods will go up. Equally business people try to control their market in order to be the dominant service or monopoly, fixing prices for maximum profit.

In summary, let me say the following and then give three additional case studies to drive home the importance of competition in nature and in humanity: A Nigerian will feel badly if the football team he or she supports in Europe loses a game. A Nigerian is sad if the presidential candidate he or she supports in American politics loses. These are competitions in which he or she has nothing to gain, no matter which side wins, but he or she will be emotionally engaged because of the way we human beings are wired.

You will ask yourself why anyone would want to commit suicide if the team he or she supports abroad loses a game. But that is how far we can go with our sentiments about winning.

To get the best from any group of humans or from a team, all you need to do is to introduce competition with a good reward for the winner. To select the best candidate for a position, all you need to do is to have the candidates compete for it, and the most suitable will emerge.

However, people with competition mentality sometimes want to win by all means. Pride, self-worth, desperation, and greed when mixed with other emotions can be very volatile. Such people want to win whether by hook or crook, and those are the people to watch out for.

So, in order to get the best results from any endeavour, you must ensure that merit plays its role.

A case study of introduction of competition to improve electricity service in Nigeria

In modern societies, the government is expected to ensure that the capacity to supply electricity to its citizens is greater than the total demand of the people. This ensures that, no matter the situation, even when some generating facilities are shut down for repairs or for other reasons, the supply will always be sufficient to meet the needs of the people.

In our case in Nigeria, supply is not adequate, and what is available is not professionally distributed to its citizens. The two main objectives that should govern electricity distribution to citizens should be (1) equity, as all citizens deserve to be treated as equal stakeholders (that means sharing what is available equally and rationally) and (2) to prioritize the strategic needs of critical social facilities like industries, universities, hospitals, and other institutions of national interest.

Based on the above premise, it is callous for the new electricity distributing companies (DisCos) to deny any section of this nation or any section of a city in this nation electricity for weeks without any remorse.

No excuse should be entertained for such indecency. If any of their facilities, say transmission lines, transformers, or the like, break down, it is the companies' duty to see the situation as an emergency and make the repairs in a few hours, so as not to deprive any section of the citizenry of this amenity. Rather, it is very common in Nigeria for certain sectors to go for long periods without electricity, as these companies do not live up to expectation. People just suffer, and there is no one the citizens can go to for rescue. These privatized DisCos have the same attitude towards work as the government agencies they took over from.

The new electricity generating companies (GenCos) and DisCos are monopolistic, opportunistic, and exploitative like their predecessors. Without competition, suppliers and providers of services tend to think they are lords over the customers, since the citizens do not have other choices.

On the part of electricity generating companies, we can only attain the necessary level of competition when the nation has greater generation capacities than is demanded. When that level of sufficiency is attained, distributing companies will seek supply from companies that are cheaper and are more customer-friendly.

We equally propose that the electricity distributing companies (those that have the high tension and low tension lines with the transformers and accessories) should be different from the electricity marketing companies, who will sell the credit cards for the prepaid meters. That way, the marketing companies can be many, and that will drive efficiency.

It is time now in our development that we should give licenses to companies that are interested in establishing facilities (distribution lines with the relevant transformers and accessories) so as to compete with the DisCos using the existing facilities. A company can choose to compete with the Port Harcourt DisCo if it has the wherewithal to have its own transmission and distribution lines within any section of the city or the whole city. When that competition exists, all the companies will sit up. The days of certain sections of the city going without electricity supply for weeks will no longer exist, and if outages occur, people will change service to the competitor, who in turn wants to increase its market share in the area.

A case study using competitive ranking of university courses to improve academic standards

Tell me why a regulatory body like the Nigerian Universities Commission cannot come up with ranking of universities at intervals in terms of the various fields of study?

Such ranking will introduce competition among the universities, and competition will enhance our educational standards over a period of time.

There was a time when we regularly received international students desiring to study in Nigerian universities. If our standard of education improves remarkably again, people will begin to rush back to study here, as was the case some decades ago.

Ranking, I know, can be politicized and corrupted, but we can easily use objectively verifiable indications to forestall such. For example, if we want to rank all the universities that offer programmes for students to study the legal profession (law), we can ask questions like:

- What is the ratio of professors to the law student population in this university?
- What is the average cut-off point of students admitted to study law in this university?

- What is the performance level of law graduates from this university in the Nigerian Law School especially in terms of percentage of students that passed the external examination?

This is not information that can be cooked up, since the answers to these questions can be easily verified by anyone.

The same applies to any other profession that needs to be ranked.

By using these objectively verifiable indicators, we can now say, this is the best Nigerian law faculty in a particular period. The same goes for civil engineering, medicine, petroleum engineering, accounting, and any other ranked profession.

Those universities that are ranked poorly in a particular year will begin to work harder to climb the ranking ladder.

We can start with a pilot scheme, where only few disciplines can be assessed, for example, law, medicine, science education, and business studies, to name a few.

A case study of private organizations sponsoring national sporting events

Currently the Channels Television of Nigeria is running a football competition for pupils of primary schools in Nigeria. Before them, Shell Petroleum Development Company of Nigeria Limited was and still is sponsoring football competitions for secondary schools.

These are highly commendable initiatives by private sector organizations, which will, in no small measure, identify some good players that can represent the nation in the future. They have done well investing in the future of our nation's football, and they are pointing the youths towards a source of employment, a source that will enhance their self-worth and self fulfilment, especially of our very talented youths who may choose to follow a career in football.

These organizations must be spending a lot of money to organize these annual competitions and putting in enormous time in the management of the logistics for the annual events.

In the case of Channels Television, this competition is an inter-school event, which means that it is the best team from the winning schools in the zones that are involved in the final competition. Obviously, this strategy means that, for example, if the best goalkeeper in the zone is not from the winning school, he would not have the opportunity to be showcased and so may never be identified for grooming to represent the nation in the long run.

It is for this reason I have always advocated that any competition that will generate the very best national team should be based on a grassroots talent hunting strategy. School competitions, be they primary or secondary, should be bottom-up: First, schools in each community should compete among themselves in what I would like to call inter-school competitions.

After that, it is not the best school that will represent the community at the next level of competition but a composite team of the best players in the community. The best team in each community in the local government area (LGA) will then compete among themselves within the LGA in the intercommunity competition. By implication, the best composite team for each community will not necessarily come from one school because the goalkeeper may come from a different school from that of the striker and so on.

After the intercommunity competition within each LGA, another composite team will be formed for each LGA within each state for the inter LGA competition. Similarly, another composite team will be formed for each state for the interstate competition. From the inter-state competition, the national team is composed. This way, the very best possible team for the nation for international competitions will emerge.

I do appreciate what Channel Television is doing at the primary level, and I do understand that the channel will not be able to handle alone this elaborate arrangement. That is why it has to be coordinated, and many organizations, both public and private, must key into it and contribute to the sponsorship.

Channels Television has started these competitive events, and now, it's time for the competitions to be upgraded in order to give our nation the optimum benefits of the events.

This competition does not have to be limited or restricted to only football; it can be implemented for all team games, including handball, volleyball, and many more.

I believe strongly that Nigeria, as a great nation, need not lag behind hopelessly in international sporting events. Nigeria needs to excel in international sporting events, where we have comparative talent advantages and the equal capacity to win gold medals in the Olympic Games.

4.10 Prioritizing our Developmental Goals

There is no nation that has all the resources to meet all its needs. This is so for Mali or Somalia as well as for the United Kingdom or United States of America; Nigeria is not different. What we need to do is prioritize our needs so that we give greater attention to those aspects that are critical in taking us to the next higher level of development.

Our ability to do this will depend on our efficiency, that is, our ability to check corruption, not only as a result of our ability to generate revenue. We can do more with the revenue we currently generate. And, if we become more efficient in terms of how we operate, we can continue performing at this level if our revenue sources decline. Even if revenue from crude oil dries up, Nigeria will not go comatose. Rather, we shall scale down our expenditures in line with our new income levels. For example, if we block all the sources of revenue leakages, like subsidy scams, crude oil theft, and the like, there is no reason we should not have more resources for development.

Since the mainstay of our economy at this time is revenue from sale of crude oil, if a negative scenario occurs wherein crude oil becomes either too cheap or gets depleted, our available income to fund education, conduct elections, carry out referendums, pay salaries, and so on will be lower. That will force the nation to experience a new reality and a new wave of adjustments. We will survive if we have planned ahead how to manage such a situation. Many nations are not as comfortable as we are today. Some even borrow money to conduct elections. If we refuse to take preventive measures now, in the future, we shall be like these poor nations grappling with belated corrective actions just for us to survive.

What I am saying, therefore, is that the opportunity we have today is peculiar. It is different from the opportunities we had some decades ago when we claimed to have more money than we could spend and eventually wrongly utilized the income. We are lucky that we can still plan how we live together without acrimony, even if it is a cheaper but more sustainable political system that would reduce cost of governance and corruption. There is no reason we should not be making investments on interventions that would rapidly develop this nation. If we do it well, other nations in West Africa may choose to have a form of union with us over time to explore the benefits of togetherness.

Let us therefore leave politics aside and plan our resources in a sustainable and equitable manner. Let us identify those sectors that can leap us into rapid advancement and give them priority funding. Research, education, electricity, transportation, agriculture, industrial development, and giving a sense of belonging to oil-producing communities, to name a few, need to be given priority. Simultaneously, we must not neglect all other sectors.

We need peace so that we will not overspend on security related issues. We need to ensure that politicians will not use our resources to enhance their selfish political capital instead of intervening to solve critical developmental needs.

We must consider the revenue we generate now as the real situation, and we should work with it, while we continue the efforts to improve on revenue generation.

It is people with lack of ideas who cannot think outside the box. Many nations and states would perform miracles if given what we have.

Over the years of profligacy, our sense of frugality has been deadened. We are wasteful, and we spend as if tomorrow will never come. We do not only spend the available income; we always justify borrowing what we do not have. At the end of the day, even what was borrowed will be wasted, leaving a burden on our future generations, who will have to pay these debts.

When we keep complaining that our revenue streams have declined, is it because there is less to loot? Can anyone imagine what we waste during our four-year presidential election cycle? Can anyone imagine what is spent by all the states for gubernatorial election?

Continually crying over revenue we generated in the past and did not use as properly as would have been expected is defeatism. All should please stop sulking and get productive.

There are nations that do not get one-tenth of what we get annually, and they are surviving and, in some cases, are doing much better than we are doing presently.

Let's get realistic, get frugal, reduce on corruption, remove subsidy, and end oil theft. In so doing, we shall be better than we have ever been.

The case against paying idle youths NGN 5,000 as monthly handouts instead of providing employment opportunities and critical national infrastructure

Rather than government giving monthly handouts to their lackeys and supporters for doing no work, it would be better to employ people for productive ventures, for which they are paid. That way, the people, one way or the other, will have contributed to earning their salaries.

Do we know that investing this money on youth empowerment initiatives like skills acquisition, scholarship schemes, business development schemes, and other schemes that will promote industrial growth will improve the quality of lives of the Nigerian youths sustainably and catalyse rapid developmental advancement?

These paltry monthly handouts will encourage people to be lazy and dependent on government largesse and give them an entitlement mentality. In the short run, these people will demand increases, since the money given to each individual is insufficient and will not address any need in an inflationary system. The implication is that a large chunk of the national income will go down the drain, since there will be less funding for real national development.

Our economy should not be managed by hardcore politicians whose interests are shortsighted and who prioritize winning the next election. Such people seem to know little about national economic management. Even if they have the knowledge, economic management is not as important to them as influencing votes during the next election.

In the Western nations where social security schemes are practiced, there are families where four generations have never worked, and their desire to work for a living has become vestigial. They're living in a situation where they and their future generations will be dependent on government handouts forever.

We have instances in some nations where some families and their past generations have not known how to work and earn their own living. All they do is depend on government for everything. I ask again, why do these political elements, who are naive and stubborn, want by all means to take the nation down this road? I ask if they know that social security schemes, even in less corrupt environments, have had unintended and negative consequences.

Is this not political rascality and playing to the gallery at the expense of national posterity? Schemes like this are easily manipulated by corrupt people. These politicians, as usual, will be very creative in stealing from this fund; a good proportion of people on the list to be given the stipends will be their cronies, political party members, ghost workers, society members, and their thugs. The list will be subjected to all sorts of crime that their minds will devise. The list will grow continuously, and the increase in size will be driven annually as a result of corruption on one hand and also because, as the national population of Nigeria grows, the demand for more people to be included on the list will increase. The implication is that there will come a time when all our resources will be targeted at settling this issue as we did during the oil subsidy quagmire. A nation where many workers are owed several months' salaries and where pensioners are owed too is not thinking of solving immediate problems but, rather, is looking for more problems to add to its lot.

While we are not reinvesting in generating more revenue and sustaining our capacity through export promotion and through the oil, gas, and solid mineral businesses, we are eager to waste revenue generated. How will we then sustain our revenue generation when we allow the vital revenue-generating industries to be dying?

We want to give our people fish always, enforcing on them dependence mentality, rather than teaching them how to fish. We are 'business people' who would rather eat up our profit than reinvest to generate more income for tomorrow and for the rainy days.

Let employment be provided for as many Nigerians as possible. Even this should be managed in a way that the private sector (who will insist on productivity) drives it.

With our extended family system, those who have employment will continue to carry the burden of their relatives. Let us therefore grow the economy so that opportunities to earn money will increase. Let us use the trillions of naira that we are planning to squander to construct roads and railways so that the people who are now out of jobs will regain employment. Let us give Nigerians twenty-four-hour electricity supply. When electricity supply to Nigerians is 100 per cent of demand (that is, being available at required quality for twenty-four hours a day), then the cost of doing business in Nigeria will reduce drastically. The major cost of running hotels, manufacturing industries, welding business, offices, churches, and so on is the cost of generating personal electricity. With improved power availability, prices will come down because many people will go into business, more people will be employed, profit will improve, and businesses will pay more taxes to government. Let us govern responsibly.

4.11 Management of Subsidy Interventions

Subsidy is an instrument governments use to regulate the prices of target products so that they are not priced out of reach by consumers or they become less competitive than imported products in a liberal market.

It costs a lot to subsidize a product, and for that reason, only critical products are so subsidized. Subsidy schemes must be applied only after the total picture is understood. The unintended likely impacts of such intervention are known, and the exposure to possible mismanagement and mitigation measures has also been identified.

Subsidy is still popular and is not in itself a bad instrument. For example, many governments subsidize the cost of fertilizers to encourage its use by farmers.

The inflationary implication of removal of any major subsidy has been a subject of much debate. Because of the possible far-reaching consequences, every school of thought is passionately holding on to its opinion or position.

In my opinion, there are many possible scenarios that can play out with the total removal of any major subsidy. We can look at the situation from a least-impact scenario to the worst possible consequence that will result in widespread anarchy. Any of these may play out, not because the subsidy removal is good or bad but because some people who do not have the best interest of the nation may seize the opportunity to escalate the issue into a crisis point, driven by other underlying issues.

I am tempted to present the extremes of possible outcomes and also provide some interventions to ameliorate the inevitable inconveniences that may ensue.

In a best-case scenario, the removal of subsidy will only result in marginal increase in inflation. The reason for this optimistic position is twofold. One, the product may be the major but almost always not only the cost component of that business. Increase in the cost of one component cannot result in astronomical increase in the cost of doing that business. Government should not allow any business owner to exploit the situation unnecessarily, even if it is a monopoly. The other factor is that, most products would have substitutes, and excessive increase in the price will make consumers go for a less preferred option.

In the worst-case scenario, removal of subsidy will result in unreasonably high inflation. This obviously will further impoverish the masses. However, the nation will save the unsustainable amount spent on the subsidy.

Mismanagement of oil subsidy as a case study

The problem of oil subsidy in Nigeria was not well understood before it was started. And before people knew what was happening, it had been hijacked by greedy businessmen who used all instruments at their disposal to blackmail, cajole, and ensure that the faulty and corrupt system continued unhindered.

A nation that pays 20 per cent of its budget to settle unproductive oil subsidy is a nation that is living on borrowed time and is heading for eventual collapse.

It is frivolous, unsustainable, and irresponsible.

What will happen when this nation's oil production reduces drastically in the course of time? Will we use all our earnings to settle oil subsidy? Who is not allowing our refineries to produce optimally? Who can attest that all oil subsidies paid for can be accounted for?

1. Oil subsidy has been partially deregulated in Nigeria in 2017. Though it is a major improvement from the situation of the past, we are still walking a tightrope. We must ensure that we completely deregulate so that many more people will invest in the construction of refineries and, thereby, produce adequate petroleum products for our use and for export.

2. A reasonable portion of the savings must be put back into revamping our existing refineries and establishing additional oil refineries. Oil refining is a critical area of the economy, and we cannot put it in the hands of the private sector alone. While private concerns can go it solo 100 per cent, government can also partner with others, where government will make minimal investments like provision of land and so forth in a public-private partnership. Many modular refineries can be so constructed.

3. Government must give all the incentives required for the private sector to establish its own refineries. Deadlines should be given for the people with licenses to commence work or such licenses must be revoked.

4. We must refine and make available far more fuel than we can utilize as a country so that we begin exporting refined products in addition to crude oil. Imagine the number of jobs that will be created, the related private businesses that will be established, and the multiplier effects on the economy if more oil refineries are built.

5. We must not only revive but also improve and modernize the railways and all mass transit systems in the country as alternate means of transporting petroleum products.

6. We must produce more electric power than the nation needs in order to reduce dependency on privately generated electric power using PMS or diesel petroleum products.

7. When many refineries (both government and those owned by the private sectors) are involved in producing petrol, diesel, kerosene, and the like or importing the same for sale to consumers, prices will come down in the long run, as competition will set in.

The quick win in this regard is the establishment of several smaller modular refineries. Give interested businessmen all the incentives required to quickly establish these modular refineries.

The modular refineries can be of any size depending on the capacity of the of the oil field and the funding abilities of the investors.

- The federal government (FG) should sell crude oil to these modular refineries at the prevailing international rates. They can get their supplies through pipelines, specialised boats or badges, land trucks, and so forth depending on the terrain.
- FG should ensure they monitor their operations by regular inspection of these modular refineries, to ensure that they deliver quality products and maintain high health, safety, and environment standards. They must not be sources of massive pollution to an already fragile environment.
- FG should provide strict operational guidelines for the refineries, especially the modular ones and should close down any refinery that habitually defaults.

- FG should revoke licenses, confiscate facilities, and auction refineries that are involved in utilizing stolen crude oil. In addition, managers of such refineries should be prosecuted.

- FG should make it easy for these modular refineries to get suitable land spaces and tax relief at the period of refinery establishment.

- Government should work towards establishing partnership with private concerns, including oil companies that own some strategic oil fields—some ten or more small or modular refineries in strategic locations within the Niger Delta—as a diversification strategy and give them a completion target of not more than ten months.

- Government should deregulate the petroleum market. Government should work with the National Assembly to enact a law that prescribes the prosecution of anyone who tries, in any way, to frustrate this effort, since such person is an enemy of the nation. Effort should also be made to put in place evacuation strategies for the refined products.

4.12 Sycophancy in Governance

I just saw a publication in which a highly placed Nigerian referred to one of the political leaders as very honest and is now accusing people who are asking for evidence that the individual is qualified in the first place for the position as bad, desperate, and so on. The first thing that came to my mind was, how can such a highly placed person refer to someone who, in the first place, came to power through deception as very honest? There are presidential and gubernatorial position holders who will do everything in this world to remain there, and I understand. Leaving the position at this time is instant imprisonment.

But come to think of it, what is the yardstick for adjudging someone as honest? Is it that you pick some characteristics and overlook others in coming to that decision? Are nepotism, deception, oppression, intimidation, and other such acts expected to be displayed by honest people?

My concern is not with the political leaders; it is with Nigerians who falsely praise people. We are willing to praise-sing, so long as crumbs are falling off the table into our mouths. Most sycophants are so sentimental that it seems they believe what they lie about.

The rationale for criticism is to make people see the negative aspects of their character; reasonable leaders will work on improving those aspects when they know their weaknesses. My people say that those the gods have decided to destroy will never be allowed to change but will remain mad and adamant until they meet their doom. Besides, most of these leaders are surrounded by leeches who deceive them with their creative sycophancy.

No person is perfect, and every human being will have his or her weaknesses. Wise leaders should actively encourage objective advice or criticism to enable them to continually improve. We urge our leaders to understand their weaknesses and seek continual improvement and not be stubborn, exhibiting arrogance.

Should we excuse sycophancy because some leaders hate criticism and would rather sack any follower who tells him the bitter truth?

4.13 Mismanaging Communications, Propaganda, and Dirty Politics

Lies, propaganda, and politics must not be allowed to come together. When they do, they are more potent than several Boko Haram bombs. They have the capacity to ruin any nation.

Effective communication aimed at providing information blended with persuasion is the best way to make people accept change peacefully. Use of force, blackmail, and manipulation are confrontational tools that make people temporarily comply. But their use is not sustainable.

Effective use of communication tools is always beneficial in convincing people to change their taste, fashion, religion, political party, or lifestyle, among other things.

In primitive times, people were forced to comply with certain standards, including religion by the use of force, threat of violence, or manipulative use of superstitious beliefs.

Modern technology has enhanced political awareness, and people now ask questions and demand answers. The world is now a global village, and the era when a cabal mentally imprisons a group of people is fading into the past, as the efficacy of tactics used to ensure such enslavement is greatly reduced. Those who are still living in the past and are arguing that people should not be educated are living in a fool's paradise.

I know that every technology has its own limitations, as propaganda and Internet fraud are some of the ills that we now have to contend with. Political propaganda is a new craze among political fraudsters. It is fraud in the sense that people obtain patronage by fraud.

Anyone who thinks that one can expand a religious base or get elected to political office via the use of force, manipulation of facts or lies, or threat of violence is simply dreaming because it is not sustainable.

Anyone who cannot adapt to the new reality and refuses to change cannot survive in this world.

Any organization that still relies on the use of force, manipulation, or violence to compel people's compliance is in trouble, as only extinction is its final destination.

Sycophancy is deeply rooted in our political system. Some people, even though they are mediocre and inadequate, try to remain relevant through sycophancy. Others feel the best way to block out competition and insecurity is to promote and encourage prejudice, misinformation, and discrimination against people who are different from them. Yet many feel the best way to secure their future is to accumulate unwanted assets from the commonwealth, no matter who suffers as a result. Acute greed, selfishness, and the continual issuing of lies and propaganda to deceive people are also symptoms of greater underlying societal issues.

Clearly these are all signs of maladjustment or mental disorders. Victims of these vices suffer greatly and require support from all. For me, we should sympathize not only with the victims but also with those who are so 'sick' as to subject people to such victimization.

Emotional manipulation has always been with humankind. Women and men use it a lot with their loved ones. Children use it a lot with their parents to get favours. Considering current economic hardship; terrorism and related assaults; and the renaissance of racial, religious, and ethnic discriminatory tendencies globally, many crafty politicians worldwide are now applying and exploiting these emotive strategies. They are using deceptive persuasion, emotional propaganda, manipulative control, and measured intimidation to get people to vote them into power. They go to great lengths, and they have successfully gotten the masses so emotionally charged that many people seem to have abandoned reasoning and good judgment.

This tactic is working, and it is not likely to stop until people learn their lessons and begin to demand evidence and not empty rhetorical falsehood.

It will not stop until people look at politicians not in terms of where they come from or look like but in terms of what they have achieved for other people in the past.

Don't tell people that you will feed them if elected. Tell them how many you have fed in your little corner in the past. Show how compassionate you have been in the past.

Don't promise to construct roads and other social amenities. Show them how many small community projects within your capacity you have done for the poor in the past.

Don't tell people that you will create jobs. Tell them how many people your small business has employed in the past or what you have done with resources placed under your control in the past as a politician prior to the election in question.

Don't tell them you are not discriminatory. Tell them how many from other tribes or religion work with you or have benefitted from your help in the past.

Our populace need to be politically educated and savvy in order for us to beat this desperate group in their game. Without that, we are going nowhere but chasing shadows.

Social media has been used for good, and it is also enhancing crime and other social vices. It can easily be used to expose ills and in so doing destroy overambitious leaders. It can also enhance the prospects of good men who would otherwise not be known and would therefore not succeed.

By implication, social media is effective in exposing the truth. However, it can be misused to scandalize the innocent. We must, therefore, be thankful for this new technology, but we must not accept propaganda. It is best to test information before we join in a chain of gossip and rumour-mongering via social media. Remember that the Bible asks us not to believe every spirit but to test them, since some of them are from the pit of hell. A good proportion of information peddled on social media is lies, and some bits of 'information' are half-truths manipulated to achieve desired effects.

No matter the skilfulness of the dirty public relations or propaganda employed, the best you can achieve is to make people temporarily see a goat as a lion. In a short period, the pack of lies will fall apart, and people will see the reality. Usually, the negative reaction that follows equals the levels of deception people have experienced. Therefore, the truth is that nothing is gained in the long run, and often, something is lost and regretted.

In politics, good people may easily be demonized. Sometimes, while the leader still maintains high morality, this leader's friends—those who depend on that leadership—will go out of their way to attack opponents, without the leader's knowledge, thus ensuring the leader remains in power and they continue to benefit from that power. If they know that their leader is too decent to rig an election, then they will work behind the leader's back to ensure victory by all means possible. Some humans are so desperate we can kill to win. We blackmail; we falsely accuse our opponents to disadvantage them. Sometime ago, I gave an analogy that some Nigerians are willing to literally dig up the goalpost in a football match and relocate the posts just to prove that you scored in the wrong place.

In a community enmeshed in impunity, it would be wasteful to seek redress in court, literally speaking. It looks too simplistic, but the frequency with which judgment changes as you appeal to higher levels indicates some cause for concern. This analogy is sequel to the election that was carried out and won by Chief M. K. O. Abiola on 12 June 1993. Another example is when the powers that be declare an election inconclusive if early results coming in indicate that they have lost; they simply go ahead and cancel the whole election, declaring it inconclusive.

Any society that is governed by cult groups, gang members, or even lawless vigilantes has taken several steps back to primitive living. This is true whether the governing powers be youth cult groups or fanatical religious groups, as is the case in some parts of north-eastern Nigeria.

Village vigilantes, politically motivated groups, secret societies, and the like all have one thing in common; they rely on fear as a weapon of control of the populace. To them, human life is not of great importance, and the punishment they give for offences, wrongs, perceived grievances, open opposition to their rule, and even threat emanating from an individual or groups is elimination by death.

Politics is a high-stake high-investment competition where the losers are left standing all alone, without supporters; fund replenishments; or, usually, settlement. In many cases, the aspirants invest all their resources and even borrow for the event.

The implication of losing is depression, bankruptcy, loss of self-esteem, and many such things. That is why politics is very murky in Nigeria, where people get desperate and are ready to even kill to realize their aspirations. They see politics as war, where either you win or are down and out. To them, it is a 'do or die' affair. Is it, therefore, not a surprise that some politicians provide weapons to their youths to eliminate dreaded opponents? Is it because of this mentality that all instruments are employed by some politicians to win the game? To them, all is fair that ends well in their favour.

4.14 Impacts of Rumour and Gossip in the Society

- A problem shared with a gossip or a bad friend is not half-solved; it is twice problematic.
- False sympathy is what a gossip gives you in exchange for details! (Dr Noel Ihebuzor)

- Problem gossiped is problem doubled. (Godwin Norbert)

I will use a case study to explain the impact of rumour and why rumour and gossip should always be avoided. But first, I have picked something from the Internet (https://www.quora.com/What-is-Triple-Filter-test-of-Socrates) that is attributed to Socrates. Kindly permit me to use it here to illustrate a point:

In ancient Greece, Socrates was reputed to hold knowledge in high esteem. One day, an acquaintance met the great philosopher and said, "Do you know what I just heard about your friend?"

"Hold on a minute," Socrates replied. "Before telling me anything I'd like you to pass a little test. It's called the triple filter Test."

"Triple filter test?"

"That's right," Socrates continued. "Before you talk to me about my friend, it might be a good idea to take a moment and filter what you're going to say. That's why I call it the triple filter test. The first filter is truth. Are you absolutely sure that what you're about to tell me is true?"

"No," the man said. "Actually I just heard about it and …"

"All right," said Socrates. "So you don't really know if it's true or not. Now let us try the second filter, the filter of goodness. Is what you're about to tell me about my friend something good?"

"No; on the contrary."

"So," Socrates continued, "You want to tell me something bad about him, but you're not certain it's true. You may still pass the test though, because there is one filter left, the filter of usefulness. Is what you want to tell me about my friend going to be useful to me?"

"No, not really!"

"Well," concluded Socrates, "If what you want to tell me is neither true nor good nor even useful, why tell it to me at all?"

Now my fictional story to demonstrate the impact of rumour and gossip is presented in the subsection that follows.

A case study on the distortion of information passed on orally

Names and characters in this story are fictional and do not represent anyone now living or who lived in the past.

The setting is a village in Africa about thirty years ago. Chief Wagu is sixty years old and village head of Waguama. He believes that every woman primarily belongs in the kitchen and the 'other room'. He cannot stand any woman who thinks otherwise. However, he is suffering from high blood pressure.

Mrs Alala is a woman in that village. She is a retired widow and a former teacher and has chosen to relocate to the village. She has been championing women's liberation and equality to men for several years, and she will not tolerate any man who does not think she is as important as he is.

Chief Wagu has heard about Mrs Alala's attitude and has made up his mind to put her in her place in this village he is heading.

One day, he decides to confront her when they meet on the way. He fumes. 'Lady, why are you passing by me without saying your greetings? Do you know who I am?'

She replies, equally angrily, 'What stopped you from greeting me? Do you know who *I* am?'

This infuriates the Chief, especially as he is with a number of other chiefs and many admirers. In anger, he asks her to come back immediately and apologize. The lady comes back but tells him that he is behaving like a primitive man and that he will see what will happen from now on.

In his rage, Chief Wagu's blood pressure shoots up, he collapses suffering a stroke and falls to the ground. Chief Wagu recovers reasonably in the hospital but with a bent face and begins rehabilitation with the help of physiotherapists.

The lady is arrested by the village vigilante, who accuses her of witchcraft.

***

The following oral transmission of what happened ensued:

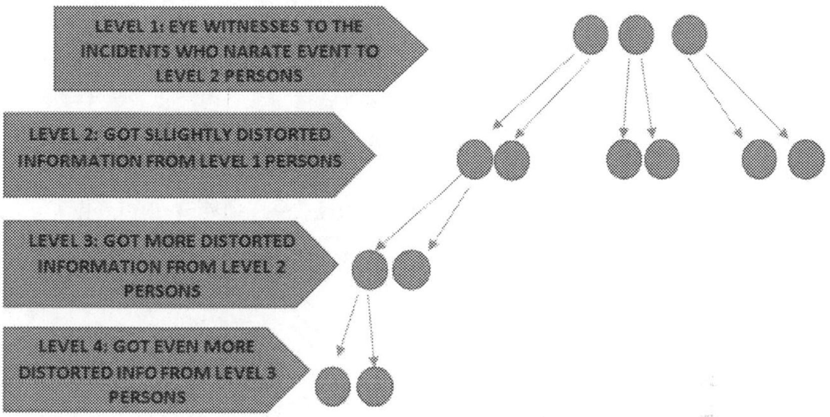

Fig. 4.1: **Likely distortions associated with oral transmission of information.**

Those who were at the scene of the conflict (level 1 persons—eye witnesses) narrated the story to the first group of listeners, stating more or less what happened.

Those first listeners (level 2 persons) narrated what they were told to others depending on what they decoded according to the emotions that were dominant in them. Some would say, 'The lady told the chief, "For insulting me, you will see," and the Chief fainted.' Others were more adventurous, saying the chief wanted to slap her, and her juju slapped him, and that was why his face was now bent.

When the level 2 persons told the level 3 persons, these distorted stories. The level 3 persons then took the information to the level 4 persons, where they further distorted the news. At that level, people heard news like, 'The chief died immediately. The witch told him to die.' Others say things like, 'The lady confessed when she was arrested and flogged by the vigilante that she killed her husband and many people when she was a teacher and only ran to the village when they wanted to burn her alive.' By this point, rumours upon rumours told how powerful the woman was as a witch, how she had killed many people in the village, and on and on.

The essence of this narrative is that rumours are never the true versions of the information. Rumours have always been distorted by the information being passed down orally.

This phenomenon of distortion of news passed down orally from person to person has been known to science for a long time and was not my invention. But I have equally demonstrated it using all forms of news items in many of the conflict management workshops I have carried out within the Niger Delta area.

4.15 Trust and Loyalty Issues in Politics

- It is not only followers who betray their bosses. Bosses also betray followers, and partners equally betray each other sometimes.
- Loyalty is often earned. You can only expect sustainable loyalty if you show respect and love to your subordinates.

Leaders must have some knowledge in the field in which they are operating, but they do not have to be technical experts. Technical expertise belongs to the senior 'lieutenants' working with a leader. The leader's major task is to motivate these experts to perform at their best and coordinate the operations so that there is optimization towards achieving organizational goals. Leaders should, instead be strategic thinkers, a strength that, when it comes to leading, is more valuable than operational expertise. The ability to apply knowledge is more important than having the knowledge. The duty of the leader, therefore, is to apply the knowledge available to the experts (assistants) in solving emerging or existing challenges. Leaders need good advice from their assistants in order to perform well, since they cannot be experts in all fields.

The quality of assistance leaders get depends on the type of experts they engage. Some leaders give greater priority to mundane considerations like zoning, friendship, ethnicity, religion, club membership, and the like than they do to professional competence. People hired not for their ability or technical knowledge but for their relationship with the leader cannot give what they do not have. They thus resort to sycophancy in order to keep their jobs. But the leader, in the process, underperforms. Leaders who do not have the character and emotional maturity to hire based on qualifications are stuck with continual lower levels of performance; simply put, they have to manage with assistants who lack the ability to make necessary improvements, given that the leader in his/her incapacity is not only unable to recruit the best but cannot change incompetent and sycophantic subordinates.

While it is true that loyalty is important in high-stake leadership environments like politics and other highly financially rewarding arenas (since overly ambitious people can try to stab a leader in the back), we must know that loyalty without competence equally will result in failure. A leader should know that, as a human being, he might easily get sucked into a cabal trap, where he gets all the advice from a kitchen cabinet whose agenda may be different from his and that of his entire followership.

It is easy for the trained mind to identify sycophants. A leader can predict their advice, as it will always tilt towards what the advice giver thinks the leader will prefer to hear instead of the truth. Sycophants will not give options or possible implications of choosing various options. They profess more loyalty than is expected of them. They spend more time providing advice, encouragement, and support on issues personal to the leader than on issues that pertain to the assignments they are given. They also show a lot of selfish traits in their dealings with their own subordinates. The truth is, they are equally the first to abandon a sinking ship and try to move on to the next leader when change occurs. Do not always blame the sycophants; some leaders hate opposition. But any adviser who has never had the opportunity to oppose the opinion of his leader over the years is, simply put, a sycophant. This is because people differ, and it is through disagreements, dialogues, and brainstorming that best or sustainable ideas emerge.

If a leader's decisions are often opposed by the followership, then that leader needs to look inwards because it is possible that he is not getting the best advice or that he is pushing away good advice due to sentimental reasons. The duty of every good leader is to create a positive legacy by providing selfless service using shared vision that will improve the welfare of his followers. All other considerations are secondary to this. Instead of disliking those who criticize him constructively, he should befriend them, as an environment that allows for open discourse will challenge him to work harder and, in the process, bring out his best. Leaders at every level should please note the above in order to excel.

Many innocent politicians, by virtue of the camp they belong to, suffer as casualties in the game as a result of envisaged political disloyalty. Many more than the leaders and their dependents lose their appointments and source of income when the courts or other factors bring about leadership changes. This is because, in politics, the demand for loyalty is total. Some politicians even go the extra miles to secure such loyalties in form of cult membership, oath of allegiance, and so on. The murky waters of politics are so dangerous in Nigeria that some decent men prefer to stay away. But the question is, for how long? Is it not only when these men who stay away go in and become active politicians that things will begin to improve?

We must equally understand that, no matter how respectful and loving you are to your senior, equal, and junior partners, a small proportion of them may still be planning your downfall for inexplicable reasons, some of which may include jealousy, greed, resentment, past experience, vengeance, or your perceived arrogance, to name a few. Those are the people you must be wary of. They are in every population, just as there was a Judah among the disciples of Jesus Christ.

Not every time disloyalty occurs is it the result or the fault of the boss. Sometimes, disloyalty takes place for reasons beyond the comprehension of the boss. And this is sometimes the case when communication is poor among the partners.

It is difficult to identify such persons in the organization, and it is the grace of God that can continue to help you forge ahead even with such saboteurs.

The best approach a boss must always apply is to be friendly and loving to all. Love all as you love yourself, communicate effectively, do not discriminate, and pray or communicate with God often. After that, leave the rest to God because God handles the rest after you have done your part.

4.16 Improving our Electoral Practices

The implementation of popular decisions made by the majority of the people is the backbone of democracy. That is why they say the minority would have its say, but the majority gets its way. This is applicable depending on whatever issue is involved. Voting is applicable in choosing who will occupy a political office or when bills have to be passed in the assembly houses. It is applicable in resolving controversies and disputes in social organizations and in any situation when majority decisions are required.

Getting to know the majority choice of the population of a large nation like Nigeria is cumbersome and expensive. The process is also susceptible to manipulations that can give incorrect results.

These two factors require that we continually improve our electioneering processes so that we reduce costs, reduce rigging, and control other electoral malpractices.

In a true democracy, it can be assumed that the character of the president is a true reflection of the character of the average citizen. This is because the president is chosen by the majority of the people.

Let me accept that there are some exceptions to this rule. Some candidates may deceive the electorate into thinking they think like them using unrealistic and false promises to win their votes. Such false representations abound.

Elections provide a basis for disagreements. Usually the parties we choose to support hold the positions we have taken in the various disagreements. However, those positions are based on objective and sentimental reasons.

The more we control our emotions, the more we will find out that our choices are indeed similar and that we ultimately have the same needs and same interests. What every citizen wants is a government that will improve his or her quality of life. Those everyone should choose to be our leader should have nothing to do with who is his or her brother or sister; every Nigerian wants food on the table, good schools for his or her children, constant electricity, jobs to keep body and soul together, and good transportation, among other basic need.

No matter how emotional we are at the beginning, even going to the extreme to resist election failure, we will always be grateful to any government that improves our situation. If, however, a government takes us for a ride, promising us things it knows fully well it will not deliver, then subtle emotions change to heightened emotions, and in outrage, people say and do things they later regret.

However, the electorate, when so deceived, will vote out the person who deceived them during the next round of elections.

Let me add that, in these days of propaganda, social media hype, and public relations manipulations, a deplorable person or even a complete fool can become the president. And this person's character profile may not necessarily be the true reflection of that of an average citizen.

An election is a leveller. The presidential candidates of the various parties; the national opinion leaders; and everyone else, including the beggars who were lucky to get the permanent voters cards (PVC) in the case of Nigeria, all have only one vote each. Politics is the national game, and democracy is the platform. It is a game that always ends with a winner and some losers. It is difficult to have a win-win outcome because of the greed of politicians. People talk of magnanimity after winning, but it is mostly rhetoric, as the planning for the next election (war) starts immediately after the swearing in.

Despite the fact that people invest huge resources during elections, not everyone will win. Despite the huge benefits accruable to the winners in a corrupt polity, the losers need not resort to violence. People have no plan for failure during election, so when they eventually fail, they always pass through a stage of denial and refuse to accept the results.

Those who want the nation to burn because they lost elections do not mean well for anyone. We do not have another nation, and so we must either live together or sink together. Politics and elections will continue as long as a nation exists, and so every election is a battle in a continuous war, where the parties may change but all opposition can never be vanquished.

I would like to ask some questions on how we can improve with regards to conducting free, fair, and affordable elections. We spend fortunes to conduct elections. The aggregate of what we spend in a general election by the government, the politicians and so on, is probably bigger than the entire budget of some small African nations. And yet our elections still aren't conducted very well. So I ask:

How can we reduce the cost of elections?

Should we increase the intervals?

Should we look for cheaper and more recyclable materials?

Should we go full-scale digital and use voters' cards for all the activities?

As for the latter, it follows that the initial high cost would involve purchasing infrastructure and, after that, we'll have only the cost of maintenance and replacements.

For the sake of our dear nation and also because this is the nation we will bequeath to our children from one generation to another in line with posterity, we must take the risk to do what all serious nations are doing. But we must prepare well by ensuring we are ready technologically before we go that way.

As we move from the outdated manual election management to a more modern, Internet friendly, and digitally embedded process, we will need competent hands. Already in Nigeria, organizations like the banks and the Joint Admissions and Matriculation Board (JAMB) have gone digital successfully.

4.17 Religious and Ethnic Terrorism

Terrorism is as old as humankind. It started with primitive wars aimed at invading peaceful people to enslave and take over their belongings. Sometimes the aim was also to forcefully convert them to a different religion other than the one they knew before they were captured.

It is now difficult to understand where religious and ethnic issues end and where political issues begin. To many, it is all mixed up, and if you do not belong to their religion and or their ethnicity then you cannot lead them. Though there is improvement, ethnic and religious hatred comes in many forms, and such vices still exist. The jobless youths are the instruments some people use to promote such hatred for people they perceive to be different from them. We should think deeply on how we can end hatred, prejudice, and the continued killing of Nigerians—all of which hide behind any excuse such people can come up with.

The heart of humanity is desperately wicked, and wicked people do not just justify very terrible acts; they convince their followers to support their actions. Killers therefore become heroes to some people, and many are willing to sabotage the progress of their nation either because they have been brainwashed or love to domineer. Good people are hated, hunted, and destroyed. Even from time immemorial, progress comes with positive change, and change is often violently resisted.

The truth is that there is deep-seated ethnic hatred in the nation. Some people seek every minor excuse possible to kill targeted groups. Until we understand that even twins differ, that there is beauty in diversity, that intolerance and conflict take us backwards in terms of development, and that impunity is primitive when it comes to hatred, true unity, progress, and peaceful coexistence will remain a mirage.

The common man is the victim when the political class chooses to behave like cult gangs, eliminating opponents and establishing or protecting their political territories. The common man is the victim when the ruling class chooses to sponsor terror in the land, using religious and or ethnic sentiments to instigate the people to fight themselves. The common man will be the victim when all these conflicts escalate and predispose us into executing a proper war, and those who instigated it, along with their families, will be the first to run away from the nation at war.

The common man has always been the victim, even when the working class disagrees on how to share the national cake and chooses to confront each other through national or localized strikes. The common man always bears the brunt and is always used to escalate and sustain the oppressive situation that does not allow him to progress.

The common man implements the sinister decisions of the mischievous leaders, whose only interest is to continually corner for themselves the entire commonwealth.

It is only when the common man knows his power that the political class will begin to listen to him and no longer use him.

There are many forms of terrorism sponsorship—provision (financial and material needs); protection (concealment of the identities of and hiding the terrorists); guidance (technical and other advice to make them effective); and moral support (any other actions aimed at motivating them including praise, criticism, of those fighting against them, and sponsorship of negative media campaigns). The truth is that every sponsor of terrorism is a terrorist.

Man can wipe out a whole clan to keep a secret or can kill and destroy a whole nation just to hide a corrupt act. There are many instances in which corrupt people have set buildings ablaze because a probe is about to take place and they needed to cover their tracks. It is true, therefore, that the heart of man is desperately wicked.

The content and the 'spirit' of insurgency changes from place to place and from time to time. Wherever it is, though, it involves loss of lives and destruction of facilities, including historical heritage or economy-boosting sites. The communities that are peaceful today may not be so tomorrow, and those that have conflicts today may be the peaceful places in the future.

If funds for the rehabilitation of war-ravaged places are not well thought through before disbursement, such funding can, in itself, become a source of another conflict. This is especially true in cases where a certain sector corners the funds, to the disadvantage of others affected or when corruption sets in when it comes to how the funding is utilized.

I do not know what made the dinosaurs go extinct several years ago, but I suspect their destruction was not self-inflicted. It must have to do with some environmental changes they could not easily adapt to. However, human beings are highly adaptable. With our high intelligence and adjustment capacities, we have captured every environment on earth, and we live successfully in most. I suspect, that in the case of man, the major reason we may go extinct one day will have to do with our inability to control our negative emotions, which some people call sentimentality or foolishness.

4.18 The illegality of Homosexual Acts

There is a wave of demand sweeping the world that homosexuals should be allowed to live a normal life without intimidation and oppression. They should be allowed to live their lives with freedom if they are born different from the rest of the people. Many nations have given such people the freedom to express the lifestyle unhindered. Others, like Nigeria, have enacted laws that make homosexuality a criminal act. My position is that, though the world is becoming more liberal and many deviant behaviours are now being allowed to be expressed freely and openly, every good citizen must obey the laws of their land. So, if an act is considered a crime in a society, then good citizens cannot go against the laws of the land but can continue to advocate for change. Another way to look at it is that those who are Christians, for example, are expected not to be homosexuals because it is against the dictates of the Bible. The Bible states the following:

> Thou shall not lie with mankind as with womankind. It is abomination. (Leviticus 18: 22)

> If a man also lie with mankind, as he lie with womankind, both of them have committed an abomination, they shall surely be put to death, their blood shall be upon them. (Leviticus 20:13)

Based on the above biblical commandments, it will be wrong for someone who is a Christian to be a lesbian or gay. Should we excommunicate homosexuals from the church? Never! Why? Jesus Christ loved sinners, and it is by bringing them close to you and continually praying and preaching to them that you may have the chance to change them for good. While they should be in the Christian fold as other sinners are, they must strive to change, and they cannot take up leadership positions, since that would enable them to negatively influence the Church. This is the same way, any self-confessed and unrepentant person against any of the stipulations of the Bible like do not kill, do not steal and so on should not take up leadership position in the Church.

The fact that homosexuality is a deviant act is not disputable. God, through nature, created humankind male and female. Most organisms are so created male and female. Nature wanted the two sexes to form a pair. Anything contrary to the plan of nature is deviancy. It would be abnormal for a male lion or tiger or any other organism to prefer to mate with its type of the same sex; that is abnormal.

People with deviant behaviours, require understanding and not castigation but they must seek help. I think that professional counselling will help them readjust.

This chapter has looked at a number of critical social issues of our times and commented on them. In some cases, the author has tried to take a position, whilst in some others, the reader is left free to take a position that is in keeping with the principles of truth, decency, and justice. In a few other cases, positions have been taken, driven largely by considerations of religion and faith. The reader may not agree with all the views expressed here. Where the views expressed here elicit lively debates and reactions from the reader, then the chapter would have succeeded in its intentions of allowing me to express my views and challenge some conventional views.

5

Conflict and Peaceful Coexistence Issues

5.1 Predisposing Issues to Criminal Behaviour

Wildlife is usually associated with raw violence. In the jungle, life often comes to a sudden and cruel end. You must be ready to kill to survive. You must be ready to kill even your type if necessary to survive. Life in the jungle is war. Luckily, humanity largely now lives in civilized societies, and human beings are not expected to kill one another in order to survive. Death as a result of assassination, armed robbery, kidnapping, and the like is not acceptable, but human beings still kill their fellows as beasts do. All forms of killing of man by man are criminal except during wars. We live in societies that are governed by laws for the good of all, and so that level of jungle and primitive life is outdated for the good of all.

Some people do bad things in this world. Though it is depressing, the world is what it is because, without bad things, we would not recognize the good things. People know when they do bad things because human beings have consciences, which kind of guide them, and this is what makes the world a liveable place. The world is progressively changing for good because of law and order in the various societies. Now people progressively know that those who do bad things will get punished. Impunity is gradually being eliminated in the world, but as everyone knows, the long journey seems to have just started.

What then makes people bad? Six reasons broadly account for bad or deviant behaviour in men and women.

- *Greed or selfishness*—Those who are selfish or greedy will commit crimes, especially those types that will give them more of what they desire. Such persons then engage in acts like stealing, taking bribes, committing advance fee fraud, and so on to gratify such negative impulses. They know that taking your property will make you feel badly, but as far as they are concerned, solving their own problems, securing their own happiness and well-being, and things like that are what matter to them. Their actions make the victims feel badly, and sometimes their victims go as low as committing suicide. But as far as they are concerned, it is a jungle—'a dog-eat-dog world'—and they survive at the expense of others. To them, the end justifies the means.

- *Negative emotions*—These include anger, hatred, jealousy, envy, desire for vengeance, resentment, and the desire to inflict pain on the object of such negative emotions. Some people are so obsessed with vengeance that they devote a good chunk of their time trying to settle past scores, rather than making personal progress with their more progressive and beneficial life goals. Human beings wallowing in these emotions may do bad things and later regret their actions.

- *Poverty*—Poverty is another reason that bad deeds are committed, and this is especially true when it includes hunger. When people are desperate to move out of terrible circumstances, they are more likely to fall to the temptation of doing desperate things. Boys join bad gangs without knowing the implications and can no longer leave the group after they have joined. Often they are forced to commit crimes, and the gang keeps the evidence to blackmail the individual. The evidence is released or exposed to the society if the individual changes his or her mind and wishes to leave the group later. Girls join prostitution rings and try to psychologically compensate themselves with a delusion that all is well if bills are paid. A combination of poverty and greed can produce monsters in people indeed.

- *Drug addiction*—This plays a major role as the fourth reason why people do bad things. Addiction makes people become confused as to the best ways to behave. Drug addiction makes people become desperate. Especially when they need some dose, they will do anything, even if it means killing to get the needed drugs to remain high.

- *Upbringing*—This is a critical aspect of value embedding, and it is the fifth reason I have chosen. People who grow up in environments where doing bad things is considered normal will have no remorse committing crimes. It is difficult to convince someone not to defraud others if he or she grew up in a place where stealing or extorting money from people for survival is considered normal, and the criminal who makes it big as a result is celebrated. Gradually, the value systems in the world are deteriorating. Progressively women getting nude in public places or showing their nude pictures over the Internet is becoming a normal thing. A young pretty lady was considering showing her nude pictures on the Internet with the flimsy excuse that she will not be young forever, and this is the time to get the best out of the world. People openly discuss and are proud of how they cheated on examinations without any remorse. Others don't seem to even consider it a crime to solicit agents to help them write their examinations. Do we therefore still wonder why the quality of education is deteriorating? In many societies these days, youths find it normal to insult and disrespect elders, and they feel no remorse for doing so.

- *Yielding to violence*—This is the last reason, and it is the vehicle to the prosecution of wars and the extreme activity of conflict. The more violence a people are exposed to, the more such people will have debased their value systems and de-sanctified humanity.

Two possible ways, among others, that can be used to reduce these crimes are, firstly, to stop impunity and encourage rule of law, and secondly, to practice our faith, especially the Christian faith that truly encourages love for each other.

5.2 What is Conflict?

* ❖ Conflict comes from unacceptable difference between what is reality and what is desired—in needs, in values, and in expectations within an individual or a group and with others.
* ❖ So long as people differ from one another, there will always be disagreements no matter the relationship. This includes inter- and intra-community relationships; intra- and international relationships, parent-child relationships; and relationships between teachers and students, bosses and subordinates, friends, enemies, and all other existing relationships.
* ❖ Conflict and violence are not synonymous, though sometimes they are used interchangeably. However, conflict can be violent or non-violent. It can be destructive and painful or constructive and useful.
* ❖ Conflict can easily become violent when structural violence (economic exploitation, racism, sexism, oppression, hunger, and poverty) exists with great impunity.

Conflict could be as a result of the following factors:

* ❖ Disagreement on how to utilise scarce resources at stake (money, land, objects and franchises)
* ❖ Territories at stake—physical territories (community, home, office, and so on) and psychological territories (area of responsibility, personal privacy, status, identity, and the like)
* ❖ Principles at stake (moral values, political ideologies, religious beliefs, personal reputation, and so on)

❖ Relationships involved (threat to existing or potential relationships; power juggling; personality clashes; prejudice; and violation of expectations such as trust, violence, abuses, and the like)

Conflict-generating circumstances abound, and people always experience conflict. Conflict is a natural part of life, and when it is well managed the win-win outcome results in better and more sustainable relationships.

❖ We sometimes feel conflict towards inanimate and other objects that we see as our source of frustration
❖ We sometimes feel conflict against people we do not know, as is often the case among road users or politicians we do not like.
❖ We have conflicts with government, institutions, spouses, and family members that we see as our source of frustration.

How we manage such conflicts depends on our level of conflict management skills and who we are conflicting with.

If the conflict is with a boss or a law enforcement person who can discipline us, we tend to apply avoidance as a way to de-escalate the conflict. That is, we accept being wrong and apologize even when we are right.

On the opposite end, if we are more powerful and can discipline the other party, we tend to apply threat and intimidation, even when we know that the fault is ours.

However, neither approach resolves the conflict. Both only make the conflict subside, and the loser, over time, may choose to fight back and confront the situation. At that point, the conflict has moved into a confrontational mode, and a fight ensues.

The best approach to resolving all conflicts is problem solving, where both parties or either party initiates dialogue to reach some compromise and, at best, collaboration for a win-win outcome.

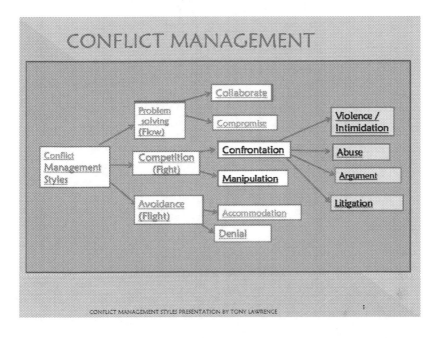

Fig. 5.1: **Conflict management.**

5.3 Issues to Consider in Managing Conflicts

Different sources of conflict give different textures to conflict. For me, there are four principal sources, namely:

- Class 1: Conflicts as a result of different preferences and different expectations
- Class 2: Conflicts of core values and principles
- Class 3: Conflicts for resource and power control
- Class 4: Religious conflicts

My humble estimation is that all conflicts have the potential to easily escalate into crisis if not well managed, and Class 1 conflicts are more easily resolved than Class 4 conflicts. The reason is simple; parties in Class 4 conflicts are driven not necessarily by transient earthly rewards. They often find it difficult to dialogue because religious instructions are not often flexible, and adherents to such religions would find it difficult to accept a compromise position that is contrary to the stipulations of their religion. This is because most religious instructions are rigid, and any deviation is seen as sin.

In reality, however, human beings are equal and free. Fundamental human rights provide that everyone's right ends where the other's starts. That implies that, while you can practice your religion, you cannot demand that another human being must practice yours or must stop practicing his or her own religion so that you will find it easier to practice yours.

If every religious person understands that just as he or she is free to practice his or her own religion, so too is the other person free to practice his or hers, then there will be less conflict.

The good thing is that most conflicts are not religious in nature, and even when they have religious coloration, religion only heightens other underlying differences and is not the major reason for the conflict. Most major conflicts are of classes 2 and 3, and because they are equally emotive, often they easily escalate into crises or wars if not well managed.

Mediators and the parties involved in the conflict must understand what they are dealing with in order to devise interventions that will make inroads and eventually result in win-win resolutions.

5.4 Conflict Escalation and Management

A fire incident involving a house can be easily controlled at the early stages with firefighting equipment. So too are cancer cases detected on time. Many natural phenomena follow the same path. Early detection and interventions are more likely to solve the problem or save a bad situation from getting worse. Political, community, ethnic, sectional, and religious conflicts are other examples. At the early stages, they are more easily managed and resolved. However, if these conflicts are allowed to fester and escalate, they get to crisis stages and consume either or both parties. When people lose during conflicts, their egos and pride are deflated, and they become motivated to seek revenge or keep the conflict alive in other forms.

Conflicts often escalate because of bystanders who have other motives. They encourage the continuation of conflicts but will be the first group to decamp when their principal loses out in the conflict.

- Must a conflict be win-lose?
- Can't we go for a win-win?

CONFLICT ESCALATION & MANAGEMENT PROCESS

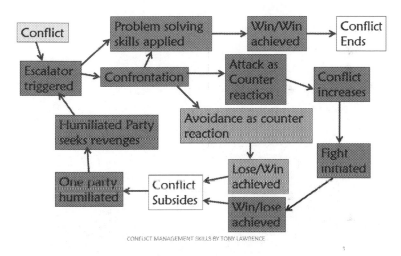

CONFLICT MANAGEMENT SKILLS BY TONY LAWRENCE

Fig. 5.2: **Conflict escalation and management.**

Figure 5.2 explains how a conflict can either be managed effectively or allowed to eventually escalate through poor handling.

Parties in conflict must sit down face-to-face and have an open-minded heart-to-heart talk if they want a win-win outcome. They should ask each other what they really want and how they can achieve mutual benefits.

Those who are angry do not understand the value of negotiation and dialogue until the anger begins to subside. Though it is not easy, we must show restraint and apply wisdom always. If this is not done, the conflict will escalate into crisis and seeking peaceful resolution will become more difficult. That means that continuing the prosecution of the conflict until one person loses physically, financially, psychologically, or otherwise in a significant manner will become increasingly more inevitable.

People with abundant common sense seem to be few, considering the regrettable actions many people take on daily basis. Some say that, when the gods want to kill a person, they first make the person mad. It might not be correct that gods have that much potency, but the saying has a lot of meaning. In the height of anger, hatred, loss of pride, and similar emotions, we become too emotional to think rationally, and the judgments we make at such times may be impaired. Everybody can be affected, and everybody has his or her moments of 'madness'. I have mine too.

5.5 Application of Conflict Management for a Win-Win Outcome

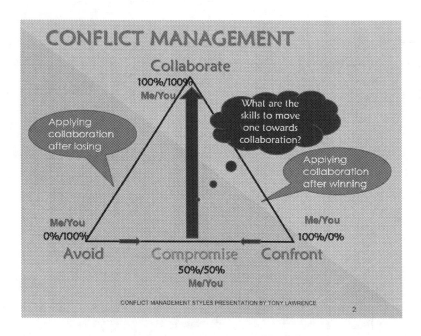

Fig. 5.3: **Conflict triangle. An illustration of how collaboration benefits both parties.**

The illustration in figure 5.3 shows that, when you apply avoidance (left-hand side of the triangle), you sacrifice your interest so that the other party wins, and you get 0 per cent of your needs or interest satisfied in the conflict. If you confront and win in the conflict (right-hand side of the triangle), then you satisfy 100 per cent of your demand from the conflict since the winner takes all. However, for a win-win a middle ground is desired and dialogue, along with give and take, is the required attitude. The best that can happen in a compromise is 50 per cent going each way.

My perception is that avoidance, confrontation, and compromise are all in the same one-dimensional continuum, where avoidance is on one side and confrontation is on the other extreme while compromise is the middle ground. Through the strategy applied, the outcome may go anywhere within the continuum, which is a zero sum form of sharing.

The best outcome in any conflict is to push out of the restrictive one-dimensional platform to a two-dimensional platform that allows for greater exploration and break away from the zero-sum restrictive envelop. The picture shows that, at the best of collaboration, both parties in the conflict can get all their needs met in a win-win outcome —that is, the parties getting 100 per cent achievement both ways.

I would like to further illustrate this with a simple case of managing post-election conflicts.

The winner would need to be magnanimous in victory and make overtures to the losers and carry them along so that the conflict will end. If not, the conflict would continue in the courts of law until it goes to supreme court.

The losers should also be able to seek dialogue with the winner so that they can recoup some of the expenses and also end the bickering and bad blood.

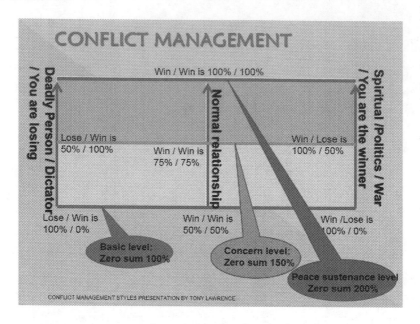

Fig. 5.4: **Conflict square. A more complex expression of the benefits of collaborative strategies.**

The illustration in figure 5.4 shows a three-level strategic platform. The basic level is a zero sum arrangement with a combined maximum of both parties meeting their expectations from the conflict. The explanation given for figure 5.3 (the triangle) still applies here.

The key strength of the figure above is that, with the use of collaboration, a win-lose outcome can be transformed into a win-win, and a win-win means that the needs and/or interests of all the parties in the situation (as much as possible) have been taken care of. The more an outcome is a win-win, the closer the cumulative benefits get to satisfying all the needs and/or interests of both parties (200 per cent).

A good professional who is not at his or her best or who is handling a very complicated conflict with difficult parties can attempt to operate at the second level, which I have called the 'concern level'.

A well-researched and well-handled mediation should seek a win-win, with each party getting all they wanted from the conflict.

This figure is versatile because it explains why someone can choose to use avoidance, for example in a situation where a person is asked to carry out instructions by a soldier during war or by an armed robber. It also demonstrates the need to bluntly refuse and confront if you are asked to do something you know is a crime and/or against your religious principles.

And it explains the need to always seek win-win outcomes in every normal relation conflict.

Do we accept wise counsel at such times when we are in the heat of conflict? Probably not. Do we seek wise counsel when our 'heads are cool'? Yes. But often, and unfortunately, the situation has, by then, deteriorated. At such times 'had I known' becomes a familiar phrase.

When arrogance, anger, and intolerance colour a conflict, belligerence, violence, and regrets all become the expected set of outcomes.

Transforming our win-lose election competition outcomes to win-win by all the parties will enhance peace and harmony in the nation and in the various states. There will be collaboration when the winners show magnanimity in victory and the losers are good sportsmen.

I will give another example to further illustrate how a possible win-lose outcome can be transformed into a win-win.

Two neighbouring communities may be disputing ownership of a land boundary. One party wants to use the land to build a secondary school. The other party wants the land to serve as a sports complex so that their youths can play football there. While some youths in both communities want to go to war, others want to commence litigation in order to claim the land. After all, the land in question is strategic and large, and it would be shameful and degrading to give it up without a fight.

Both options—war and litigation—will be costly, and so someone asked for the two sides to, rather, see a good mediator. The mediator was able to help them abandon their respective positions and concentrate on their needs and interests. Afterwards, both parties understood that it was easy to proffer the option of using the land for a school with a sports complex. That way, the needs of both communities would be met. Everyone had moved from a win-lose mode to a win-win mode with the possibility of each party getting 100 per cent of its needs met, resulting in an aggregate outcome of 200% percent.

5.6 My experience with a lady driver as a case study on how to manage conflict

It was an afternoon in 2009, and I was driving along the one-way section of Ogbunabali Road near Garrison Junction in Port Harcourt. A lady was reversing onto the road from a parking lot and was not checking her back. She ran her car into mine, despite all the blaring of horns to prevent the accident.

We both got out of our vehicles to inspect and ascertain the damage done. I observed that there was no damage to mine, but there was a little dent to her car and her rear lights were broken.

My assessment of the situation was as follows:

1. She was at fault since she reversed into my car despite warnings.
2. My car was intact, so there was no requirement that she should pay for repairs.

Thus, I advised her to always drive carefully so that she would not cause more problems for herself in the future.

However, I was surprised that she refused to let me leave, demanding that I repair her car, which my car damaged. This attracted the interest of passers-by, who intervened and advised her to go on her way because she was at fault. Nonetheless, the lady would not budge.

At this point, I had become infuriated and asked, 'Lady, are you insane?' And the conflict escalated, this time not only because she was demanding that I pay for her car to be repaired but also because, according to her, I had called her a madwoman. She swore that she would make me suffer for saying she was mad and that, since I think she was mad, she would behave like a madwoman to me.

The traffic along Ogbunabali Road had piled up, since we would not leave the road to enable a free flow of traffic, and I had to invite the traffic policemen at nearby Garrison Junction to intervene. Despite the ruling by the policemen that she was at fault, the lady refused to bulge.

Many people pleaded with her to take control of herself and let go. And after a period, she entered her car and drove to the side.

My impression at that time was that she had decided to let go and the conflict was resolved. I, therefore, also entered my car and started going on my way. As usual, when I drive, I often use the rear-view mirror to see who is following. It was to my amazement that I noticed the lady was still following me. I decided to take streets I knew she would rather not pass, but there she was still following my car.

Then it became clear to me that this lady had not let go and was still spoiling for a vengeful confrontation. I had to call a senior police friend to ask what I needed to do in the circumstance. I knew fully well that, in 2009, Port Harcourt, and indeed the Niger Delta, was embroiled in militancy. My police friend advised that I should drive to a nearby police station and report the matter. As I drove into the police station, the lady also drove her car into the station. I then approached the policemen on duty and reported what had happened and how the traffic police at Garrison had intervened, but the lady was still following me all over the place.

The lady replied to the police enquiry by stating that we had had an accident and she'd asked me to repair her car. Instead of repairing her car, she told the officers, I had described her as mad, and it was her intention to show me how mad people behave. At this time, the lady was using her palm to hit the floor at the police station. She did this several times, forcefully vowing that she would not let go.

The police officers tried to confirm from me whether I had actually described her as a madwoman. I replied by saying that her action in the police station, hitting the floor several times without any respect for the office and the officers, had confirmed that she must be mad.

Assessing the situation, we now found ourselves in, the police officers chose to use the mediation strategy to resolve the conflict.

They took her aside and spoke with her for a long while. After they had finished with her, they also took me aside and spoke with me. They advised me never to describe anyone as mad because such behaviour can bring out negative emotions in some people, as people react differently to abuses. They added that I was lucky the lady had not attacked me violently at the scene of the accident for abusing her. It was at this time that I explained to them that I had not actually call her a madwoman at the scene of the accident but had only asked if she was insane.

To this, the police officers said it did not matter how I had said it. What was communicated could be decoded by individuals based on the circumstances and their perception of things.

They then advised that I should apologize to her and, if possible, support her in any way I could for her to repair her car.

Haven spoken to us separately, they brought us together again and asked us not to escalate the simple matter unnecessarily and that we should forgive each other and let go.

I then cued in by apologizing to her and explained that I had never said she was mad. I had only asked if she was, as she was refusing all the advice that the passers-by had given to her based on what had caused the accident. I also gave her about three thousand naira, which I had in my pocket at the time, for her to add to what she had and replace the broken rear light.

This gesture was well appreciated by the lady, who also apologized for the way she had acted and assured me that she had forgiven me and that the conflict between us was all over.

I then thanked the police officers for their mediation and left the station as a free man again.

The lessons here are:

1. In a conflict situation, always avoid the use of abusive language, as it will escalate the conflict.

2. If nerves are frayed as a result of your unintended action, always be ready to quickly apologize for such actions before they result in confrontation by the other party.

3. Try to amicably negotiate disagreements using assertive but friendly means to communicate with the other party during a conflict.

4. Involve a neutral mediator if adequate progress is not made.

5. Insisting on your right, without the willingness for compromise or desire for win-win ending may result in a physical fight, which could result in a fatality.

5.7 The Woes of Violence and War

Violence can be referred to as the use of physical, psychological, or verbal force against self or others. It can take many forms, ranging from mere hitting between people causing bodily harm to war and genocide with huge numbers of fatalities. Violence can also be verbal, psychological, emotional, and spiritual as well as physical.

Structural violence includes pervasive poverty, exclusion, hunger, exploitation, intimidation, oppression, fear, and the like. Even if structural violence is not physical, it can easily degenerate into physical violence.

War on the other hand is:

*   A state of prolonged violence
*   A major conflict involving two or more groups
*   Often fought to resolve territorial conflicts

Wars can be acts of aggression to conquer territories or loot assets, though at times they are fought for national self-defence.

In a number of instances, wars can be fought to suppress parts of a nation that wants to secede.

Some key issues to note about violence:

- Violence begets violence.
- Violence is counter-development.
- Use of violence is jungle justice.
- Might is not right.
- It is not a sustainable solution.
- Violent leaders are feared, not respected.
- People will attach the misdeeds of despotic leaders to their future generations.

Violent conflict destroys community heritage (imagine the level of destructions that take place in modern wars, where a whole community can be levelled with series of bombardments).

Violence affects the sustainability of community development, where all historic sites, buildings, tourists' sites, social amenities, and economic infrastructure are destroyed.

Violence affects the physical and mental health of the people affected.

Violence disrupts children's education.

Violence results in untimely deaths, of several people in some cases.

Violence equally places a long-term trauma in the hearts of the people.

Violence brings about the emergence of cult groups that commit crimes.

Violence increases poverty.

The Inverse Relationship Between Development and Violence

Development

Violence

Presentation by Sir Tony Lawrence: Community, Inter Relations and Conciliation Initiative

Fig. 5.5: **The inverse relationship between peace and violence.**

There are no benefits that can be attributed to violent conflicts in any community, and most times, the major factors that predispose violent confrontations in societies and nations include the following:

1. Insensitivity of bigoted and despotic leaders, impervious to empathy and concerns or interests of the other party
2. Arrogance, a delusional sense of importance, and an unfounded sense of entitlement embedded in the megalomaniac disposition of a leader who constantly desires to take over and control the resources and rights of others
3. Rationalizing and elevating human 'parasitic behaviour' to become acceptable as part of our core values and making such behaviour(s) enviable to the ordinary man and seen as worthy character traits for emulation by others
4. Leaders rationalizing and deluding themselves into believing that crimes of covetous extortions are good as long as the victims are different from them in terms of ethnicity, religion, or belonging to a minority group

5. Leaders' rationalization that greed is not greed when resources are not enough to satisfy the needs of everyone
6. Leaders' belief that they have accumulated enough weapons to prosecute effective war, if intimidation fails

Yes, there are situations in which people who fear wars and would avoid them by all means have been backed against a wall and will die if they do not defend themselves appropriately. Such a people therefore lose nothing by fighting back.

The truth is that many people have mental challenges, and some even enjoy war conditions because it gives them the opportunity to express their sadistic tendencies, where they kill the unarmed and innocent. Such people fan the embers of war, making utterances that will heat up the polity and hoping the war that has deluded Nigeria for about forty years will happen if they keep at it.

However, war is not desirable and will adversely affect the people:

1. A good number of people who are not indigenes are likely to move away to safer places. They will go, along with their businesses, income, job opportunities, and so on.
2. Even indigenes who feel unsafe will relocate to other states.
3. Schools within the area and at the outskirts are likely to close down, and this will increase the percentage of dropouts or children who will not have the opportunity to acquire education and other skills.
4. Farmers will not go to remote farms, for fear of attacks, and that will aggravate food scarcity in the near future.
5. Poverty will be more pronounced, since job and business opportunities will be minimal.
6. The people living in the affected areas will have war mentality and may suffer psychological trauma.
7. Most government income and funding will be diverted to manage security issues and rehabilitation after the war, instead of being used for progressive sustainable development.
8. If the problem persists, there will be no economic activities.

Additional problems if there is prolonged full-scale war include the following:

1. The youths in those areas will not enjoy any meaningful education and will not have reasonable and employable skills. They will become angry and desperate and engage in crimes when they cannot get employment to 'keep body and soul together'.
2. Without functional schools in these areas, the affected children over time will be illiterate. They will lack education and skills suitable for future developmental requirements and will likely become menial labourers, gatemen and the like. This will defeat the sustainable development goals and aspirations.

Nature and some groups are busy building up the ecosystem and community civilization and infrastructure respectively on one hand. And on the other hand, nature is destroying the ecosystem through wildfires, floods, earthquakes, and other natural disasters. Human groups are also busy destroying other humans, the ecosystems, human civilization, community, national historic edifices, and other amenities and resources through wars and other violent activities.

It's a cycle without any sustainable progress. It's all vanity, as we remain constantly busy in futility. Call it a pessimistic view of the world, but it is disheartening.

Case study: oil production sabotage by communities as violent expression of grievances

The oil business is a relationship standing on a tripod—its legs, the government, the host communities and the business investors in the industry.

Currently this relationship is debilitating and there is difficulty in the resolution of conflicts, which has reduced oil business productivity and made the industry in Nigeria operate at abysmally suboptimal levels. The cost of doing business is excessively high due to both security related costs and massive crude oil theft.

The host communities accuse the other two legs of the tripod (the government and investors) of short-changing them in the relationship. They claim that they do not get their due benefits from the relationship. They argue that, as members of the nation, they are entitled to developmental interventions even if they do not contribute anything to the national revenue coffers. And they feel enslaved and oppressed, as little is given to them when they contribute over 80 per cent of the national income. They think that, while wealth is taken away from them forcefully, what is left behind includes sorrow, poverty, a damaged and poisoned environment, and degraded sources of livelihood. They have, therefore, chosen to make the oil business environment unfriendly for optimum productivity.

The government, on the other hand, is embarrassed that this tiny component of the nation is holding it for ransom while it gives the sector so much attention. Government representatives do not waste any time in listing out what they do for this difficult group of communities. The government has given them amnesty packages, the Niger Delta Development Commission (NDDC), 13 per cent derivation payments, and the specific Ministry of Niger Delta Affairs, just to mention a few. As far as government at the centre is concern, these people already have more than they deserve, and like Oliver Twist, they are still asking for more.

The investors, for their part, know that the communities they operate in are not getting the dividends of the oil operations as expected, though they do not say so. They know that things would have been different for these communities if they were in a developed nation. They will tell you openly that they pay their taxes and operate within regulations and so do no wrong as operators or businesspeople. It is not their responsibility to develop these communities; that is the responsibility of governments (local, state, and federal). As far as the investors are concerned, they do not fail to obey the laws of the land and so are good corporate citizens. They will also tell you that they try on their own and within their capacities to "drop" little things here and there in the host communities so that they will not be caught as scapegoats in the web of conflicts.

As in most conflicts, each of the tripod legs seems to make a good case as a disputing party. In addition, and none is willing to put itself in the position of the other so as to better appreciate where that party is coming from, and the conflict festers and pesters.

Also like in every conflict, the disputing parties have taken difficult positions, and it seems resolution will be far from coming. However, like every conflict, if the disputants step out of their rigid positions and try to identify commonalities and general interests that everyone is striving for, then this conflict will be resolved in no time. Before this issue can be sustainably resolved, however, each party must identify what it is currently losing as a result of the position it has taken in the conflict. Each party must also use the following guiding principles:

- Is the situation fair to all?
- Does my position infringe on anyone's fundamental rights?
- Would I be happy with the situation if I were in the position of the other party?
- What is the implication of my position in the long run?

Now, let us rank the parties in terms of who has the greatest power to initiate conflict resolution interventions and who is losing most in the current conflict. In my mind, the government is the most powerful in this relationship. This is because the nature and interpretation of our constitution tilts more in the government's favour. Government makes the regulations and call them the legal framework. The government is made up of human beings, and these people bring their emotional baggage to bear in the relationship. The buck actually stops at the table of government and its leaders.

The investors are also powerful but not as powerful as the government. However, they know which button to press when their core interests are at risk. A lot of times, the government listens to the investors more than it does to the host communities because the investors can choose to leave the nation if things deteriorate. If this happens, the government will be at a big loss, especially as the government is looking for more investors and not the exit of those already on ground. The signal of massive departure of investors from a nation will frighten others from coming.

The host communities are the least powerful. They are at the mercy of the government because the government has all the instruments that can enforce cohesion and compliance. The communities are equally made up of people who have differing and selfish individual agendas. It is, therefore, easy for the other groups to divide and rule them in perpetuity.

With regards to who is losing most in the current conflict situation, I think the government is the greatest loser. Why do I say so? The duty of government is to develop and secure the nation. If more than 30 per cent of its income is lost as a result of conflict, then the people as a whole lose through the government. People in Government may be gaining in the short run, but posterity will judge them harshly. Governments (local, state, and federal) do not operate in isolation and so they are perceived harshly by their contemporaries and have no respect from or good reputation with them over time. Leaders who are despotic truly are not loved by the oppressed. They may claim to be good leaders, but in the true sense, they are simply rulers and not leaders. Many of the people they rule dislike their policies and their negative disposition around issues.

The investors also lose because they will be operating in a suboptimal manner with lower levels of profit. Even if they choose to leave, they will be selling their assets at much lower than the actual market values. They may be exposed to unnecessary and unwarranted security risks. They will be paying huge sums to protect themselves, and this will cut deep into their profits. The insecurity will cause asset and product theft and vandalism to be more rampant and further reduce profitability of their investment. The reputation of the investors will be in tatters on the international scenes and among their peers.

As for the host communities, they too will lose a lot as a result of the conflict. To start with, the little benefits that were trickling in will dry up. This conflict unfortunately involves vandalism, and the attendant effect is massive oil pollution, which violently impacts the ecological systems of the environment and destroys the people's source of livelihoods. These are very massive losses, even if they try to rationalize that they have been down all the while, suffering the same environmental damages. By implication, this line of reasoning holds that the communities suffer the same whether oil production goes on or not and it allows the communities to be falsely guided by the adage, 'He who is down needs fear no fall'.

So what is the way forward?

I think the key to opening the door that will resolve this conflict is with the federal government. Can a listening and a caring government think that what the host communities see as little is in fact too much? Can we address the issues effectively when the target beneficiaries are not fully involved in deciding their priority projects and how such projects should be implemented?

Does anyone consider how the oil-producing communities will feel later if they were not able to use the opportunity of oil boom to spring themselves from subsistence livelihood to a people of high economic prowess, especially when most of the revenue from the 13 per cent and other resources are controlled at the state levels and not by the oil-producing communities who suffer the negative impact?

How can we ensure that benefit captors and corrupt individuals in the Niger Delta do not strip from these oil-producing host communities their rightful benefits?

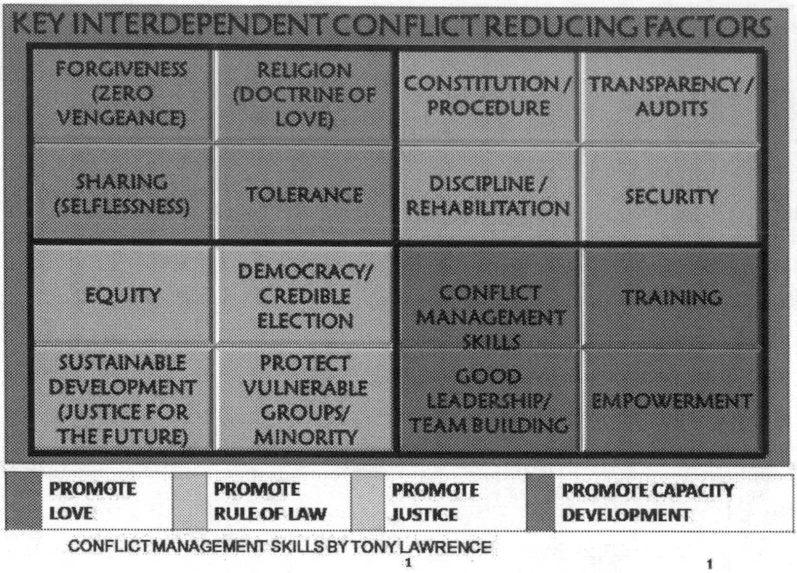

KEY INTERDEPENDENT CONFLICT REDUCING FACTORS

FORGIVENESS (ZERO VENGEANCE)	RELIGION (DOCTRINE OF LOVE)	CONSTITUTION / PROCEDURE	TRANSPARENCY / AUDITS
SHARING (SELFLESSNESS)	TOLERANCE	DISCIPLINE / REHABILITATION	SECURITY
EQUITY	DEMOCRACY/ CREDIBLE ELECTION	CONFLICT MANAGEMENT SKILLS	TRAINING
SUSTAINABLE DEVELOPMENT (JUSTICE FOR THE FUTURE)	PROTECT VULNERABLE GROUPS/ MINORITY	GOOD LEADERSHIP/ TEAM BUILDING	EMPOWERMENT
PROMOTE LOVE	PROMOTE RULE OF LAW	PROMOTE JUSTICE	PROMOTE CAPACITY DEVELOPMENT

CONFLICT MANAGEMENT SKILLS BY TONY LAWRENCE

Fig. 5.6: **Key factors for reducing conflict.**

The illustration in figure 5.6 explains in a holistic manner the key interdependent factors that can enhance rapid national development through effective conflict management.

Sustainable Development and Sustainable Advancement Issues

6.1 The Concept of Sustainable Development

The United Nations World Commission on Environment and Development published the report *Our Common Future*, commonly called the Brundtland Report, in 1987. This report contained the commonly used definition of sustainable development as follows:

Sustainable development is development that meets the needs of the present without compromising the ability of future generations to meet their own needs. It contains within it two key concepts:

- The concept of 'needs', in particular, the essential needs of the world's poor, to which overriding priority should be given; and
- The idea of limitations imposed by the state of technology and social organization on the environment's ability to meet present and future needs.

—World Commission on Environment and Development, *Our Common Future* (1987)

Sustainable development can equally be described thus:

Sustainable development is the organizing principle for meeting human development goals while at the same time sustaining the ability of natural systems to provide the natural resources and ecosystem services upon which the economy and society depends. The desirable end result is a state of society where living conditions and resource use continue to meet human needs without undermining the integrity and stability of the natural systems.

World Commission on Environment and Development, *Our Common Future* (1987)

The modern concept of sustainable development was largely obtained from the 1987 Brundtland Report, though the concept had been applied at lower scales in individual efforts, like as it was used in sustainable forest management and in the environmental concern initiatives of the twentieth century. The concept later expanded into considerations for economic and social development issues.

Non-renewable resources cannot be used sustainably, no matter how much frugality is applied, since the resources involved are finite and will be exhausted one day.

Sustainable development has since then developed to include social inclusiveness and environmentally sustainable economic growth. It is for this reason that Agenda 21 for sustainable development added information availability as a necessity for development, integration of all environmental and social concerns into all development interventions, and broad-based participation of all affected to be involved in decision-making as critical success factors for adoption by nations.

Sustainable development goals

By September 2015, the United Nations General Assembly had adopted the "universal, integrated and transformative" 2030 Agenda for Sustainable Development, a set of seventeen sustainable development goals (SDGs). The goals are to be implemented and achieved in every country from the year 2016 to 2030.

René Passet, in 1979, had proposed sustainable development to be based on three components—the environment, the economy, and society. However, other components subsequently added include culture, institutions, governance, equity, and more.

The sustainable development goals (SDGs) intervention—a set of seventeen "global goals" with 169 targets facilitated by the United Nations—is a broader intervention than its predecessor, the millennium development goals. The philosophy behind SDGs is rooted in the quote of the previous United Nations Secretary-General Ban Ki-moon: 'We don't have plan B because there is no planet B.'

The seventeen SDGs with 169 targets cover many sustainable development issues, including ending poverty and hunger, improving health and education, making cities more sustainable, combating climate change, and protecting oceans and forests.

Below is the list of the seventeen SDGs (UNDP in Nigeria2016):

1. No poverty
2. Zero hunger
3. Good health and well-being
4. Quality education
5. Gender equality
6. Clean water and sanitation
7. Affordable and clean energy
8. Decent work and economic growth
9. Industry, innovation, and infrastructure
10. Reduced inequalities
11. Sustainable cities and communities
12. Responsible consumption and production
13. Climate action
14. Life below water
15. Life on land
16. Peace, justice, and strong institutions
17. Partnership for the goals

The primary concern of *Some Governance and Peaceful Coexistence Issues for Sustainable Advancement* is the need to discuss how to apply sustainable development principles in order to achieve sustained advancement as a nation at micro levels.

I have developed two concepts that I believe all developmental projects should be subjected to at the conception phases.

The first discusses some sustainability filters and enhancers that interventions must be subjected to and the fact that there are three categories of such interventions. In other words, interventions can essentially be grouped into three categories:

- Those that are undertaken principally to raise revenue though boosting employment (for example, establishment of industries or export crop farms)
- Those established primarily to provide a social service (for example, the establishment of schools or hospitals)
- Those established to achieve both objectives (for example, transport business)

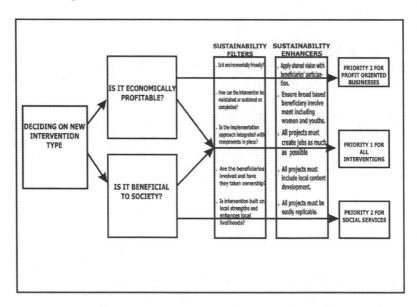

Fig. 6.1: **This illustration provides another perspective to look at the sustainability of proposed interventions.**

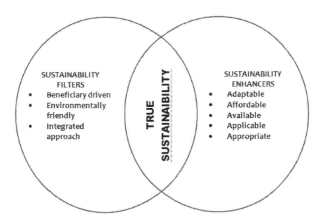

It is important to subject every new developmental intervention to two sets of criteria:

1. Sustaianbilty filters
2. Sustainability enhancers

Sustainability criteria examines issues that would enhance project or intervention success after implementation, be it a cassava processing factory, a new classroom block for a school, an electricity producing generator for a community, a potable water scheme, or any other project.

The first set of questions (*sustainability filters*, which are critical factors that must be considered before an intervention can be considred sustainable) will assess whether the proposed implementation process for the intervention will:

1. Ensure the participation and involvement of the target beneficiaries in the planning, implementation, and management of the project
2. Ensure that possible health, safety, social, and other environmental impacts of implementing the intervention have been evaluated and mitigation measures put in place towards addressing implied negative impacts

3. Ensure that the intervention has considered all the critical success factors in a holistic manner and is using an integrated and coordinated approach both at the supra-system (system and its external environment) and subsystem or intra-system (system and its internal environment) levels

The other set of questions (*sustainability enhancers*, which are factors that, when present, make interventions more sustainable) are aimed at assessing and addressing the following, which I have termed the 5 As:

1. *Adaptable*—Intervention should be easily modifiable and usable in other circumstances that beneficiaries may be exposed to. Interventions that can be easily replicated will be more easily mass-adopted
2. *Affordable*—Intervention should be cheap enough to attract more investors and ensure mass production, replication, and adoption.
3. *Available*—Interventions (as well as spare parts) should be available if others want to replicate them. You need to assess whether the people will be able to secure spare parts to maintain the project on completion.
4. *Applicable*—Interventions should be able to effectively resolve and address the developmental problem that it intends to address. The intervention should be relevant to the needs of the people.
5. *Appropriate*—Is the technology relevant to the level of development of the beneficiaries? For example, an intervention providing a public water scheme whose source of power will be the national electricity grid will not be useful in a location where there is not constant electricity supply. An alternate power source must be built into the project to make it functional. Beneficiaries need to understand how to operate the intervention, and if not, it is important that their capacities are built during and after the implementation of the project.

Based on the above, an intervention that has considered both the sustainability filters and sustainability enhancers is more likely to be truly sustainable.

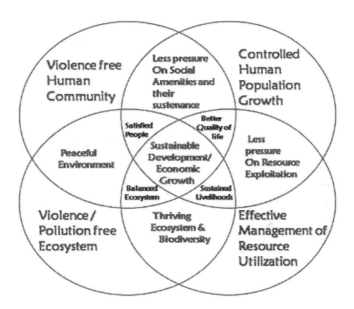

Fig. 6.2: **Four interdependent critical factors (peaceful society, unpolluted environment, wisely managed resources, and controlled human population) that together enhance sustainable development.**

The interplay of the four factors described in figure 6.2 (peaceful society, unpolluted environment, wisely managed resources, and controlled human population) results in varying outcomes as shown in the figure.

A society where all the factors are under control has enabled environment for effective sustainable development:

- Effective interplay of pollution-free ecosystem with well-managed resources will enhance a thriving ecosystem and well-protected biodiversity.
- Pollution-free ecosystem with communities that are not at war means that such societies are peaceful.

- People who manage their resources and control their human population will not suffer lack.
- Societies that are not at war and control their human population growth will have adequate amenities for its citizens.

At the inner level, the following can again be deducted:

- People who are at peace and have adequate social amenities will normally experience satisfaction.
- On the other hand, people experiencing peace who also have an undisturbed environment will be in harmony with nature.
- Those with adequate resources and unperturbed ecosystems will continue to have adequate resources for their use.
- People with adequate resources and adequate social amenities will have a better quality of life.

Finally, the core message of the concept is that satisfied people, enjoying a good environment, good quality of life, and adequate resources will obviously enjoy sustainable development.

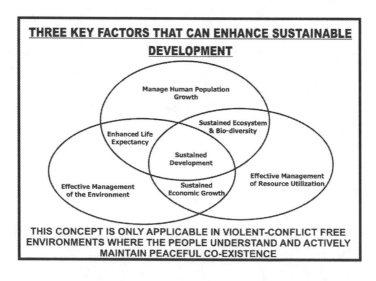

Fig. 6.3: **The benefits of sustainable development, this time using three critical factors, on the assumption that the fourth factor (peace) is a given.**

114

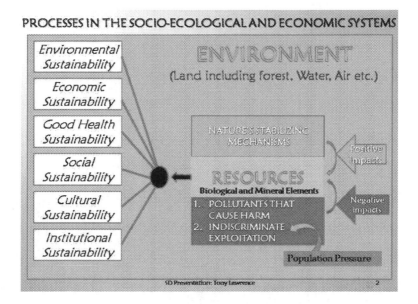

Fig. 6.4: **An illustration of sustainable development as a holistic approach in managing resources so that their exploitation does not negatively affect any aspect of the system.**

It involves dynamic and integrated management of environmental, economic, health, social, cultural, and institutional sustainability. Living and renewable resources have to be managed in a way that they are within their carrying capacities to avoid deterioration in their individual systems, as well as within the total ecosystem. Equally, non-renewable resources have to be frugally and responsibly exploited so that they serve for as long as possible.

The proactive thinking of how to innovate and actually use technology to reduce consumption and achieve minimal exploitation of non-renewable resources and also identify renewable substitute is outside sustainable development.

Combining the two aspects of sustainable development and technology is what I have called sustainable advancement.

6.2 The Concept of Sustainable Advancement

Sustainable advancement is centred on the human being, and since people cannot exist in isolation, it also looks at the total ecosystem in harmony with humanity.

Sustainable development as a concept has been around for a long time, but unfortunately most people just regard it as a buzzword that has no relevance to their everyday lives. Recent happenings in the world, however, are making people want to understand the implications of living without adequate care of the environment and other life-support resources. There are now many incidents of very aggressive hurricanes that behave as if they have scores to settle with humanity. There is massive air, water, and land pollution that is reducing life expectancy. Sea level is rising with the continuous melting of the polar ice, and many lowland islands in the world have been submerged. With global warming, some tropical disease vectors are now gradually seen at the fringes of our temperate neighbours. With the evidence of progressive depletion in the ozone layer and the attendant increase in the penetration of the ultra violet rays, I will not be surprised if ultraviolent radiation is found to be one of the actors contributing to the increasing incidents of cancer among human beings. We are equally destroying nature's resources to meet out selfish and immediate wants, and we are populating the world in a way that ensures that soon the earth will not be able to take care of the excessive population of human beings living on it.

John D. Shutter of CNN, in a report entitled 'Mass Extinction: The Era of Biological Annihilation,' stated that three-quarters of all species could disappear in the coming centuries. He reported the work of a number of scientists published in the Proceedings of the National Academy of Sciences. Gerardo Ceballos, an ecology professor at the Universidad Nacional Autónoma de México, and his co-authors, reported that nearly one-third of the 27,600 land-based mammal, bird, amphibian, and reptile species studied are shrinking in terms of their numbers and territorial range. The researchers called that an 'extremely high degree of population decay'.

The scientists equally stated that all of 177 mammal species had at least lost 30 per cent of their territory between 1900 and 2015 and more than 40 per cent of them had experienced population declines.

Another way to look at it is that the homes of most wild species, which account for the vast number of organisms, are the natural vegetation, and these areas of vegetation are being cleared annually for human use.

This may sound theoretical and academic, but life expectancy is reducing, especially in developing nations where the greater impact of these things exist. Our forest buffers are going at an alarming rate; many species of life in the oceans, forests, and everywhere else have gone extinct. This is the true reality of life, and we should begin to worry that, one day, humanity will go extinct as the dinosaurs did. Apart from these enumerated issues, humankind will obviously accelerate its own demise with the continuous stockpiling of nuclear bombs by some who think that possession of nuclear weapons gives them power and respect. Man is indeed a foolish being, and all our knowledge, scientific inventions, and ingenuity have made us even more foolish, proud, and arrogant. The way things are, therefore, it is man that shall make mankind extinct.

Sustainable development, which the world, through the UN and others are facilitating, has culminated in the adoption of sustainable development goals and associated targets.

I am, however, of the opinion that, at this point, sustainable development may not be exactly what we want. While it should not be disregarded, I think we want a more holistic and a less restrictive concept that gives greater attention to technology and science—a concept that would allow each and every one of us to think outside the box, ensuring the continuous existence of humankind on earth.

I therefore propose a new concept, which I would like to call *sustainable advancement*.

Sustainable advancement looks at the issue from a more holistic perspective (an integration of sustainable development and targeted scientific efforts to radically improve the system) and it is based on some of the following premises and reasoning:

1. Humankind is a critical factor and is contributing more than other living beings to the eventual destruction of itself and nature. We are destroying the forest systems and polluting our water bodies with gaseous, liquid, and solid pollutants. These activities are adversely affecting biodiversity.

2. Overharvesting of any resource that is self-replenishing will result in a downwards spiral in productivity and eventual extinction. This accounts for the reduction of biodiversity, along with pollution and direct destruction through other means.

3. New technology can improve productivity and enhance the continuous reduction of input items to get far increasing output and productivity. The implication is that we will not overharvest resources to get work done or satisfy the needs of the teeming masses anymore. For example, if we improve the fuel energy consumption technology well, we will require little or no fuel to drive our cars. If input reduces but still achieve the same or increased output, then increasing population on earth can be better managed.

4. While we fear resource depletion, as is the case with fossil fuel for example, we must pursue technological progress that will find greener resources to do the same work or more. That way, fossil fuel will no longer become useful to mankind, and the associated pollution and carbon emissions will equally be eliminated. The implication of this concept is that technology can play a key role in reducing the negative impacts of living in a non-sustainable manner.

5. We must understand that, while sustainable development is looking at how we can utilize resources in a way that will be beneficial to us and future generations, sustainable advancement is not only looking at sustainable development but also at other options that will finally eliminate that particular threat through invention of new and improved technology.

6. Sustainable advancement is not only looking at health, safety, and environmental impacts of our activities, it also looks at how we must continuously improve our performances, efficiency,

and the best ways to get the best results in any activity in which we are involved.

7. Sustainable advancement also looks at economics, opportunity, costs, and investment components of every activity to secure the future.

8. Science and technology was not given its pride of place in the new 17 Sustainable Development Goals (SDGS) and yet science and technology have the greatest potentials to radically enhance sustainable development and improve quality of life for humanity or tragically end the existence of humanity equally and both are critical issues. It is therefore important that humanity through the United Nations and all its agencies and all governments in the world need to actively and deliberately encourage science and technology that will enhance sustainable development and human advancement. Equally these bodies should actively and deliberately put in place laws and disincentives for any to pursue the types of science and technology that can enhance the efficacy of weapons of mass destruction. Anyone (be he the president of the most powerful nation in the world) should be punished or ostracized if he uses these weapons on innocent people. All such deliberate inventions, mass-production and use of weapons of mass destruction should be declared as crimes against humanity.

CONCLUSION

From the above it can be deducted that the application of the concept of sustainability filters will ensure that any proposed intervention on completion will be functional and sustainable. On the other hand the application of sustainability enhancers will further improve the functionality and sustainability of such interventions.

At the macro level, a drill down analysis is proposed to identify key problems to be addressed in any setting.

Finally the article attempted to advance a more progressive concept: sustainable advancement to progress us away from this not too sustainable concept that we call sustainable development since most resources we are trying to utilize sustainably are finite and will eventually be depleted with the increasing population pressure.

6.3 The Relationship between Development and Peaceful Coexistence

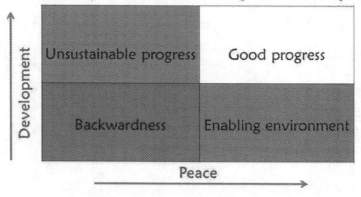

Fig. 6.5: **The positive relationship between peace and development.**

The best condition for sustainable development is when a community is experiencing the best condition of peaceful coexistence and harmony on one hand and having great developmental strides, as shown in the top right quadrant of figure 6.5.

The next best condition is when the community is experiencing peaceful coexistence without corresponding effort to develop themselves. Even if sustainable development will not be rapid, there is an enabling environment for growth and development as shown in the bottom right quadrant of figure 6.5.

The top, left quadrant shows that, if a community is developing rapidly economically, socially, and otherwise implementing infrastructure and other amenities but there is no peace, then one single devastating war will destroy all the developmental efforts made and so such situation is not sustainable.

The worst situation, as shown in the bottom left quadrant of figure 6.5 is when a community is not experiencing peace but suffering violent conflicts and, at the same time, is not making enough effort to grow itself in terms of development.

One of the key issues that had been repeated several times in this book is the futility of sustainable development if war will precede efforts and destroy achievement and take us developmentally back several years. The figure above shows that peace is a prerequisite for development.

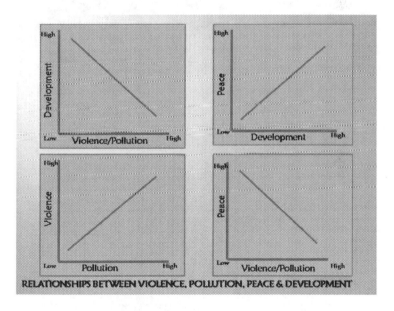

Fig. 6.6: **The relationship between development, peace, and violence and pollution as a form of violence. It is clear that there are inverse relationships between development and peace on one side and violence and pollution on the other.**

6.4 Overpopulation, Unemployment, and Other Problems

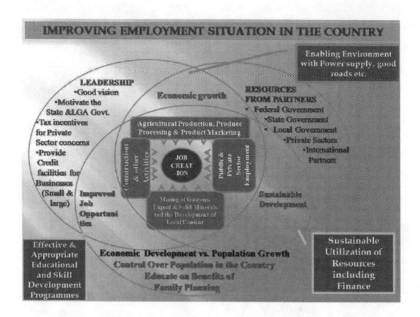

Fig. 6.7: **Some critical factors that can positively interact to improve employment in a society.**

The World Bank stated that Nigeria's population was 168.8 Million in 2012. Mathew Boesler stated in *Business Insider* on the 8 August 2013 that, at that time, the United States' population was 313.9 million. He considered the growth rates of both nations and postulated, like the World Bank, that Nigeria's population will overtake Indonesia's by 2034 and that of the United States by 2045.

The geometric increase of Nigeria's population is a good reason to be worried. According to Worldometers (www.Worldometers.info), our population was 41 million in 1955, 50 million in 1965, 63.6 million in 1975, 83.9 million in 1985, 108.4 million in 1995, 139.6 million in 2005, and 183.5 million in 2015.

The factors that increase our population are religion, historical need for children as insurance when we grow old, need for children as labour force, absence of reproductive health services, culture, and ignorance.

From 1955 up to 1975, when our population was below 65 million, every graduate of our universities had employment. Now our population has outstripped our governmental abilities to increase our facilities in terms of schools, universities, electricity supply, social amenities, and even our ability to provide employment.

While our population growth is galloping away without restrictions, our developmental growth is slow, in some instances stunted and in other situations moving in the opposite direction. That means that the future is bleak. Clearly, something needs to be done and soon.

There are university graduates who have been searching for jobs for the past ten years and more, and yet, annually, several others mature or graduate and enter the labour market. I know the psychology of the unemployed, and it takes courage and spiritualism for a good number of them not to get into a life of crime.

We know the problems that our populace is facing just to survive. Consider the risks they take in order to travel abroad in search of the elusive greener pastures. Consider the risks they take to locally and illegally refine crude oil and the risks they take involving themselves in all forms of vices.

Our developmental interventions will not be so effective, since we have a multitude of Nigerians to feed, clothe, and house.

In addition, we have a challenging corruption culture in terms of how we manage our finances, how we manage people, how we discriminate, and how we encourage mediocrity. We have the challenge of a shrinking productive national landmass, with the ever-encroaching desertification in the north, massive erosion in the rainforest areas, and continuous degradation of local livelihoods in the Niger Delta. With factors such as a thriving market for stolen crude oil, low prices that our main export commodity (crude oil) attracts at this time, and general mismanagement, our national revenue base is shrinking.

Other nations have gone through this phase too, and we can do something about it effectively if we abandon sentimental governance and face our problems objectively. The General Ibrahim B. Babangida era tried to enact a policy that restricted each family to having a maximum of four children. Though a wise policy, it has not been effective.

China and Germany, among other nations, had a similar problem and had to confront it. We too can face our problems squarely, if we want to make genuine progress roundly.

Nigeria is undisputedly making progress on an average basis, but our effort is like one step forwards, two steps backwards due to factors beyond the control of the government. This includes the uncontrolled birth rate, which nullifies any progress made.

As long as we have uncontrolled population growth and millions are added annually, we shall continue to chase shadows with regards to providing employment for all, making available social amenities cater for the needs of all, reducing poverty, controlling crimes, and effectively utilizing resources.

Obviously, there has been some progress made by the government, but what do you expect when demand is more than what can be realistically achieved?

The problem is getting worse, as every year, more hungry mouths, more unemployed youths, more youths that cannot get admitted into schools of their choices are added to the population, thereby complicating the already bad situation. Something needs to be done to avoid the 'Arab Spring' situation here.

6.5 Health and Life Expectancy Issues

Life expectancy refers to the average expected age a person will live before death in any location. This is usually affected by the genes inherited from parents, environmental conditions, and safety conditions. Factors include levels of stress, poverty, and ability to afford good health care; the availability of modern health care; levels of security; gender; and individual emotional maturity, to name a few.

Life expectancy in Nigeria is low. *This Day*, on 10 December 2016 cited the May 2016 World Health Organization (WHO) report on life expectancy data: 'Nigeria has one of the lowest life expectancy ratios in Africa and in the world; with 55 years for females and 54 years for males, standing at the 177th position, just better than only eight other countries of the world. On the average, the life expectancy ratio is 54.5 for the country.'

Considering the life expectancy of other nations, our government needs to seriously implement activities that will enable us to achieve more of the sustainable development goals.

The *This Day* report stated the life expectancy of other nations in comparison:

> In Japan, an average person will live to as high as 83.7 years, those in United Kingdom will live up to 81 years, others in United States will live up to 79 years, while in Algeria, which is an African country, the life expectancy rate is 75 years. Also, global life expectancy is at 71.4 years, which has therefore made Nigeria's indices a far cry compared to the human and natural resources at the country's disposal that could tackle factors collaborating against positive life expectancy rate.

The embarrassing thing, as reported by *This Day* is that 'even war-torn countries like South Sudan, Rwanda, Yemen, Afghanistan, and poorer nations like Mozambique and Democratic Republic of Congo (DRC) all have a higher life expectancy rate than Africa's giant, Nigeria. Meaning citizens of these countries will, on the average, live longer than Nigerians.'

In the Niger Delta, apart from the usual poverty, crude oil has been reported to have seeped into the aquifer, and the drinkable source of water may have been polluted in some areas. Seafood has accumulated a lot of poisonous substances and may be indirectly killing those in the food chain that depend on seafood as a source of food. The ability to afford medical care depends on finances available to the individual. How can a poor person manage illnesses like diabetes, kidney failure, high blood pressure, those that require expensive surgeries, and HIV, among others? To the poor, such diseases only mean one thing—sure death.

The situation, rather than getting better, is getting worse. There is thick soot now in the Niger Delta; at least I know it is now a menace in

Port Harcourt. No one has told us what is causing it. Whatever is the cause, those who on their own avoid smoking cigarettes are all exposed, and it will have one obvious impact on the people—further reduced life expectancy in the region.

I have heard some people call those who must take drugs daily to stay alive as living dead or walking dead. I have always revolted when people with special needs are so described. It is like a man lacking one essential input that is required to stay alive; with improvement in science these days, such input can be supplied from outside the system so that the individual will still have the same quality of life as when such input was naturally made available by his own body.

In the olden days, people died untimely because of minor issues like inadequate supply of insulin or uncontrollable high blood pressure. We are lucky, as science has improved life expectancy.

I have attained the stage in life during which some of these drugs need to be taken regularly, and I am lucky because, with modern science and availability of suitable drugs, life is still enjoyable. I pity our ancestors who had to die young from similar conditions, only for the people to accuse one face-frowning uncle or rugged-looking elderly aunty of witchcraft.

I would detest being seen as a living dead just because I need a constant supply of intervention drugs to live well. The lesson all must learn is that no one should laugh at the sick person because, no matter how strong you are today, you shall fall ill in the future. Do not celebrate the death of anyone because you too will die one day.

7

Other Issues

No matter how you shout to the deaf, the deaf will not hear you. No matter how you demonstrate, the blind will not see you. A similar concept applies to those whose reasoning abilities are completely under the control of their emotions. They can never be persuaded.

7.1 The Ills of Corruption and Some Ways to Reduce its Effects on National and Organizational Development

Corruption and related vices arc negatively affecting national and organizational development. Despite the fact that Nigeria is resource rich, we are currently rated as one of the poorest nations in the world. This irony is deeply rooted in the fact that corruption has become a way of life in certain areas of the economy. One of the aims of this closing chapter is stimulating people's thoughts and contributing to an understanding of the impact of this malaise of corruption on our national polity. It also intends to direct our thinking on how everyone could contribute towards salvaging the nation and all its subunits from this vice and subsequently place Nigeria on the pedestal for rapid national advancement.

To develop the key concept for this chapter, I will start by making an assumption. That is, humankind, by nature, is selfish. This natural 'survival attribute' is very evident at childhood, but as young people mature, they begin to imbibe societal values and to drop some selfish tendencies, trading them in for those that enhance the collective good of society. The tendency to be selfish has different degrees of expression in different people depending on several influences, including religion, background, poverty, culture, and genetics, among others. In some, this selfish tendency is so strong that such people are essentially very greedy in nature. Such people will embrace corruption when they see any little opportunity to do so.

I will try at this time to attempt explaining what corruption and related social malaise are. Let us say corruption is when there is deviation from the 'rule' (approved processes of doing things), usually for a selfish and personal interest. In other words, corruption is when people do things primarily for personal aggrandizement, to meet individual or subset's goals and objectives at the expense of achieving collective or group goals and objectives. This definition, you will agree, is broad. So are the many issues that come under the concept of corrupt practices.

The implication of this broad definition is then that, if any one does anything that is not in consonance with the approved processes, for example the constitutional provisions, the laws of the land, the guidelines, and other procedures put in place to foster good governance, transparency, smooth operations, and integrity, the individual is in fact involved in corruption and is therefore liable to be punished.

Corruption is not only in the public domain but applies equally to the private, corporate, and even to law and order domains. The multiple presentations of corruptions and its multidimensionality also mean that efforts to tackle it must be multifaceted if they are to succeed.

Noel Ihebuzor, in a number of blog posts, has offered additional illustrations of corruption (see references).

Aspects of corruption

Four aspects of corruption are easily identifiable. These include resource embezzlement, bribery, resource misallocation, and process abuse.

A. Resource embezzlement often refers to financial embezzlement but may affect other resources too. Finance is a key element in every organization or group, without which no organizational goals and objectives can be met. No nation can develop if its finances are embezzled or its budgetary plans are never properly implemented. Usually, plans, strategies and budgets are tied to availability of finances, which then determines the availability of other resources needed to achieve the goals and objectives of the group (be it a nation, a state, a local government, or other organization). Mismanagement of this critical element simply will result in failure of the organization or nation in meeting its goals and objectives. Resource embezzlement happens when the mismanagement is not due to incompetence but to a deliberate action by the relevant staff to circumvent the procedure or carries out his or her duty in a way that he or she benefits personally at the expense of the greater goal of the organization. The staff member, therefore, does not carry out his or her duties as stipulated. This, over time, results in suboptimal organizational performance. Resource embezzlement introduces increased cost of operations and/or poor quality performance.

An example of resource embezzlement is when an officer inflates the contract sum for a job so that he or she will get something for himself selfishly or when a contractor accepts a job below the actual amount required to properly execute the job. The implication of implementing a job below actual cost because of corruption is that the job will be poorly executed or the contractor will abandon it halfway through completion.

This is also true when a driver inflates the actual cost of fuelling a car, when a medical officer employed by the government sells drugs meant to be given freely to the populace or spends time instead at a private hospital, when civil servants decides to be trading in the office, when electric supplier employees collects bills without paying same into the organization's coffers, or when a tax collector gives fake receipts and pockets money that would have otherwise enriched government coffers. With these few examples you can see that an organization that is suffering from resource embezzlement will not be able to meet its set goals and objectives.

B. Bribery can be described as a precondition before an unmerited favour is rendered. Usually the bribe taker asks for a settlement that must be given or agreed upon before the request can be handled. You will agree with me that bribery results in awards being given to someone that is not the most qualified and, therefore, encourages mediocrity. On the other hand, competition, together with meritocracy, results in continuous improvement of performance and standards and, thereby, enhances productivity and ensures rapid growth and development. Favouritism due to inducement brings on board incompetent persons who will increase the chances of poor performance and reduced productivity. Both the giver and the taker in bribery are to be punished since, without one, the other will not function.

Encouragement of bribery results in deprivation of revenue from government coffers. This happens for example when a policeman or road marshals ask for fees less than those established for traffic violation so that the money is pocketed instead of paying it into government coffers. A worrisome development in our universities is when lecturers award unmerited scores to students not based on their performance but based on the amount of money given as bribe (sorting). An indirect bribery occurs when a lecturer forces students to buy handouts or books at highly exorbitant prices, knowing that whoever refuses to buy will fail an examination. The implication of these abuses in the long run is the deterioration of the quality of graduates we produce.

If bribery is when there is a precondition settlement before an unmerited favour is given, then it is different from a gratitude given by a pleased person. Gratitude is when someone says thank you verbally or in kind. Some organizations discourage gratification since it can be abused or misapplied. Someone who says thank you sometimes may be saying, indirectly, remember me again. However, when people work together over a period of time as contractor, supplier, subordinate, supervisor, superior, or customer, a relationship develops, and it will be difficult, even unrealistic, to insist that there should be no exchange of gifts between such people as appropriate. There can be no single way of addressing this concern (that is, rejection of all types of gifts). It is not African to reject gifts. Gifts should be reasonable and not too expensive. That means staff of organizations may accept small gifts, and they should equally give gifts like diaries, calendars, and other souvenirs to their contacts to enhance existing relationships.

C. The next aspect of corruption is resource misapplication. Apart from resource embezzlement, resources can easily be misapplied. While we can say staff members who use their duty time to pursue personal issues are guilty of resource embezzlement as well as resource misapplication. The examples given previously—government-employed medical officers who spend most of their time in their personal clinics; civil servants who spend their time trading or on other personal projects; and CEOs who divert workers from their legitimate work to do personal activities, like driving their wives, taking children to school, and handling their private businesses but getting paid by the organization—are all similar examples. Staff members who use official time on personal pursuits, such as surfing the Internet, instead of attending to customers are also guilty of resource misallocation.

People often for personal reasons change an authorized allocation to benefit whoever they favour. If, for example, someone allocates fifteen scholarship chances to his LGA at the expense of other LGAs, who instead of getting ten chances each get fewer chances, that person is guilty of resource misallocation. If however, the allocation is changed because there are not enough qualified persons in a given LGA to take up the quota, it is the duty of only the authorizing body to make the adjustment after a proposal from the action party. Changing the allocation without such authorization is the offence.

Governors or president who uses the commonwealth to benefit only their favoured sections of the country are obviously guilty of resource misallocation.

D. Process abuse is the fourth aspect of corruption. Process abuse simply means deviation from the procedure without authorization but with the intention to selfishly benefit the individual. This notwithstanding, process abuse can be a crime and at other times it can be just a violation and so must be discouraged, since even violations can easily degenerate over time to actual crimes.

A military officer who is involved in a coup d'état is guilty of a crime. Even if the regime involved is bad, corrupt, or otherwise unsuitable, a coup d'état is still a process abuse. Coup is not an approved process of changing a corrupt or lazy government, and any abuse of process must be punished.

Let us look at the lecturer who decides to help students by printing lecture notes to help them with their studies. The lecturer who sells the printout at exorbitant prices to the student is guilty of resource embezzlement. If it is the decision of the university senate to ban the use of such printout and a lecturer creates one against the senate's decision due to the plea of s student who dearly needs the write-up, the lecturer is still guilty of process abuse. What is expected from the lecturer is to make a representation to the authority that made the ban for a step-out approval. That kind of step-out approval can be given only by the same body that has made the rule in the first place. In giving a step-out approval, the authority needs to put in place checks to ensure the process is not abused or exploited.

Using another example, the head teacher may decide to increase the approved levy for the students in a school to enable the school to change a leaking school roof. Despite the noble intention, it will be resource embezzlement if the levy rates are exorbitant so that the head teacher gains financially. It is still corruption (process abuse) if financial gains by individuals are insignificant or non-existent. This is because, though the students are suffering from the leaking roof, it is not the duty of the teachers to repair school buildings.

The only way to avoid being guilty of process abuse is for the individual to secure an approval from the authority to implement the action, no matter how urgent or noble the intention is. Process abuse, therefore, is just like corruption. However, in this case, the purpose for the deviation is not due to an obvious selfish gain.

Four aspects of corruption have so far been explained, namely resource embezzlement, bribery, resource misallocation, and process abuse.

Impact of corruption on national development

The first casualty of corruption is the value system. Corruption over time degenerates, and people begin to see corrupt practices as normal. Someone once told me, showing no remorse, how surrogates assisted him to pass his examination. People like that no longer know the difference between an accepted behaviour and a crime. Some civil servants assume that it is normal for you to drop some money before they assist you. I have met a civil servant who earns a monthly salary without going to work often. You will be surprised that some people choose to forge a signature instead of going through the rigors of getting the actual signatory to sign it.

Corruption is a virus; people are easily attracted to following the crimes of corrupt people who are successful and are not punished. If corruption is permitted, then almost everyone will be corrupt.

There are vices related to corruption that give it room to blossom. One example is tribalism. People are ready to protect a son of the soil who is being prosecuted for corruption, just because he is a son of the soil or because he brought the loot home, and it benefited them. They see upright people as foolish and people who loot the commonwealth as smart since, as far as they are concerned, it is their turn to take from the national cake.

In every society where corruption is common, the rate of development is obviously impaired because the pursuit of the individual or subgroup interest erodes the rate at which such a group can move towards achieving its set goals and objectives. The implication is that leakages due to corruption result in massive sub-optimization. Two countries or organizations at par with same strategic plan and resources (say ten years ago) will not be at the same level of growth and development today if one of them encourages massive corruption in its system. Nations with adequate resources but much poverty are good examples of nations that are suffering due to permissive corrupt practices. Ghana was once a poor nation compared to Nigeria. In the eighties many Ghanaians flooded Nigeria for job opportunities. Today the table has turned. Nigerians even prefer to attend school in Ghana. At a point in the past, a strong national leader, Jerry Rawlings, introduced some shock measures, which eventually contributed to steering the ship of Ghana. Today Ghana is on its path to rapid national development, while Nigeria is still on the path of slow economic growth that cannot keep up with our ever-increasing national population growth.

Countries like China that took the approach of killing people found guilty of corruption are already reaping the fruits of that intervention with rapid development recorded. China may soon become the biggest world power the way the nation is going.

That notwithstanding, I am not advocating such extreme interventions for Nigeria, as violence begets violence and is not of God. Violence does not give room for people to change.

What then are the management interventions and consequences that would be appropriate in our situation?

I am of the school of thought that, in order to reduce corruption, disciplinary measures must be appropriately severe and enforced without fear or favour. The intention of my proposed intervention will be two-fold, first, to recover what has been stolen if possible and, second, to discourage and deter people from committing similar acts of corruption by giving strict jail terms.

I am advocating a graduated disciplinary measure. An officer guilty of financial embezzlement who is capable of refunding all the ill-gotten money should serve 25 per cent of the jail term for that offence. An officer who refunds between 99 and 50 per cent of the ill-gotten wealth should serve 26 to 50 per cent of the jail term, while an officer who is only able to refund less than 50 per cent of the ill-gotten wealth should serve above 50 per cent of the jail term. The jail term for resource embezzlement should be a minimum of two years for 100 per cent recovery and a maximum of eight years for no recovery.

An individual is guilty of corruption not from the time of the action but from the time of conception. Soliciting is as much a crime as the actual corruption. By soliciting, one is already guilty of process abuse, having sought deviation from the approved process. In the case of resource embezzlement and bribery, everyone who is involved is to be punished. Bribery is a major national malaise and must be given the strictest form of punishment as a deterrent, as is the case with resource embezzlement.

Consequence of resource misallocation should range from a jail term of a maximum of two years, a sanction, demotion to a termination of appointment, or a combination of these.

As is the case in resource embezzlement, every benefactor of resource misallocation has to be punished one way or the other. For example, if resources that should have been equitably shared to LGAs are lopsidedly allocated, the perpetrator must be punished. For the sake of equity, the resource allocation for subsequent years must take into consideration the need to address previous misallocation until equity is achieved.

For process abuse, the consequence should be a sanction or demotion or a termination of the appointment.

Apart from resource embezzlement and bribery, which must be tried in the courts of law, other offences may be tried by special committees or by the organizations or community involved (for example, community associations, committees, or clubs), depending on the type of offence involved.

Nigerians should report people who have acquired ill-gotten money, and the relevant agencies should investigate such reports to ascertain how the accused acquired the wealth. Currently, the incentives given to whistle-blowers should continue. Any ill-gotten wealth that cannot be explained must be forfeited to the government, no matter where the stolen asset is within or outside the nation.

In order to strengthen the judiciary system and eliminate process abuses, any magistrate or judge whose previous judgements have been overturned by superior courts more than three times should be investigated by a judicial body. This body should sanction, demote, or terminate such officer for incompetence or process abuse.

What is the role for existing anti-corruption agencies?

If this war against corruption will be won, bodies like the Asset Declaration Bureau, Public Complaint Commission (PCC), Economic and Financial Crimes Commission (EFCC), Independent Corrupt Practices Commission (ICPC), and so on will all have to function effectively with greater funding. Security agents should ensure that names of whistle-blowers are not given to the public so that people will be encouraged to blow the whistle on illicit activity.

What is the role of education in all of this?

I strongly believe that no new law should be retroactive. People should be informed in clear terms of both the offences and the consequences of being found guilty. That can be done through workshops, sensitization talks, and use of mass media.

Also, a key aspect of this drive will be to ensure that future generations of Nigeria will be less prone to corruption. I believe that reorientation should start at the nursery levels for children who have the opportunity to go to school that early. All Nigerian children must be educated on the ills of corruption; the need to protect our only country; the value of patriotism; the need to love our neighbours; the benefits of peaceful coexistence; religious tolerance; and the importance of reputation, honesty, integrity, and other important qualities.

To achieve this goal, education must be made compulsory for every Nigerian child, no matter what achieving that aim will take. This is a war that we must win so that future Nigerians will hold their heads high in the comity of nations.

Let me quickly state that there are pros and cons in setting up restrictions or controls in organizations to reduce corruption. Controls tend to slow down processes and sometimes restrict innovations, but establishing controls is for the greater good. A bright intervention may not come to light if the innovator is afraid that he would be accused of process abuse. However, the consequence of allowing free abuse of processes will result in massive corruption and other unnecessary risky behaviour that would expose the organization to deterioration and eventual possible collapse. New innovations or inventions have to go through the approval of the authorizing body before mass implementation in order to reduce such risks and encourage discipline.

We must sharpen our ability to sniff out corruption in our organizations, communities, local governments, states, and nation if we shall make any progress. The anti-corruption agencies, whistle-blowers, and other parties who play a role in reducing corruption will all have to work extra hard.

Most formal organizations and government already have financial regulations, laws, and the overall constitution to regulate day-to-day operations. To me, that is sufficient. What is required at this moment is strict enforcement of the provisions in those statutes.

If people know that there will be no 'sacred cows' and that no amount of bribe giving will exonerate the guilty, corruption will be reduced. Though governors and presidents have immunity, said immunity ends with their tenure. We must resist any manipulation by anybody through perpetual injunction and other means to prevent the law from taking its course. There is no need to cry foul that those being prosecuted are singled out because of their political stand when actually they are guilty.

All other social clubs, community associations, and other such groups who do not have functional constitution must update their processes to be compliant. Supervisory bodies can help by providing generic constitution, so as to avoid people bending the rules to protect their evil intentions.

A corruption-free country on its own will not result in rapid development, but it will put in place the necessary foundation or precondition for the speedy growth of the nation. For a nation to grow rapidly, there must be effective management of its resources, which will include visionary planning, implementation, monitoring, evaluation, consequence management, and so on. Who Nigeria needs is, therefore, not just someone who can fight corruption but someone who can do so while also driving our development in the right direction and working harmoniously with the other arms of government.

Can Nigeria reduce corruption to a manageable level? My answer to the question is yes. But we must have leadership commitment at all levels, from the federal level to the councillors and from the small social clubs in our villages to the big corporate bodies. Nigeria is a sensitive nation, where care is needed in implementation of delicate programmes like this. There will be massive opposition from the guilty, and so we need a nonviolent and quiet revolution. We need mature leaders to drive the process. People who think they know more than every other person and who do not consult adequately before taking decisions or act before thinking will not be suitable. People who are autocratic or extremist should not drive the process.

Nigeria can significantly outpace every African nation economically within the next ten years if we are all committed. The future is in our own hands, and as a people, we can shape our own destiny and protect our posterity.

7.2 How our Mental States Affect Our Judgements

- As humans, we are sentimental being. Our decisions are affected by our emotions, and whether we like it or not, we are often exposed to making costly but avoidable mistakes. And we not only stick to them when they are made, we escalate the consequences out of the desire to protect our pride and reputation.
- Poverty is the fuel, and negative emotions serve as oxygen. When both are mixed, violence (fire) is always possible.

The use of power by individuals, groups, and nations to control, capture, and convert others to their side is gradually becoming ineffective, as government (in national affairs) and United Nations (in international affairs) play protective roles to ensure human rights are respected and protected. Such wars may still be effective in the short run but are no longer sustainable in the long run.

The new and more sustainable strategy to change people is to fight the war in the battlefields of the mind like product marketers do. The instrument of persuasion is the new tool, and those who are good at utilizing it are more successful. Those who appeal respectfully to people's emotions are more potent and have longer-lasting effects on their targets. This is what the new school of thinking prefers and is perfecting. And this is what we need to work on, what we need to invest in, rather than acquiring more weapons of mass destruction and relying on arrogance, superiority complex, and intimidation.

Do not get me wrong. We still need to acquire some weapons of mass destruction for now as protective measures because, when people know you can fight back if they attack you, they will be reluctant to take you on or overrun you out of existence.

At the time Lord Lugard was in charge of Nigeria, our people were largely illiterate pagan worshipers. Our thinking pattern then was tied around our circumstances and limitations. Today's black people are far different from the type Lugard met. Black people are intelligent and cannot be found inferior when placed in the same environment and groomed together with other races. God has given each race some form of gifts, and white people have contributed more in the areas of scientific pursuits, while black people have excelled in artistic pursuits. I agree that, even in these pursuits, the indicators of success depend on who is setting the standards. For example, to set a standard, we must consider what each group sees as progress in science and arts. Every standard, even what we consider good or bad, must be viewed within a context, without which it might not have much meaning.

I am not saying there are no challenges. We have not made as much progress in the scientific world as white people. What I believe retarded our progress in the scientific breakthrough areas may be the same factors that are limiting our progress in our social advancement.

Some key factors limiting us include a high degree of selfishness and greed. Selfishness and greed prevent our people from sharing breakthrough ideas. People protect their new ideas so that they can benefit from them and get the credit. This is further reinforced since such ideas can easily be stolen and no credit given to the originator.

Advancement in science and in all other fields, however, is continuous improvement, each contributor building on the progress made by predecessors in the field of endeavour. People develop further on the findings and ideas of others. No nation can grow if everybody goes back to reinvent the wheel.

Everyone hides trade secrets. Native doctors, for example, will not make public the medicinal plants they use to cure people but prefer to shroud the trade secrets by pointing to interplay by ancestral spirits and the doctors' ability to fight demonic forces.

Let me now discuss related issues that affect humanity and Nigerians equally.

As a result of selfishness and greed, people's decision on what to support depends on how the action will benefit them in line with the following preferential ranking—(1) personal gain, (2) the benefit of offspring, (3) the benefit of extended family, (4) the benefit of personal community, (5) the benefit of personal tribe, (6) the benefit of people of same religion, and so on and so forth.

This tendency breeds mediocrity, as meritocracy is not allowed to thrive.

Many of us are quite emotional. Out of the three main qualities of the mind—namely, thought, memory, and emotions—those who are unable to control their emotions tend to be a lot more 'foolish'. I'm referring to foolish in the sense that we are more sentimental than required, and the judgments we make when we are highly emotional will naturally be less objective, having been affected by whichever emotions are predominating our minds at that time. Those who are very angry cannot reason effectively, and they often regret decisions they make in such state of mind. The same inability to reason effectively will affect most decisions we make when we are jealous, greedy, full of hatred, resentful, or afraid, just to mention a few emotional states that affect judgement.

The way emotions affect our reasoning is the same way they affect our memory processes. Many people are known to store information selectively depending on the emotional attachment given to the idea when it occurred. Emotions cause us to have selective memory retention.

Without objectivity, rather than people making progress, they may retrogress. Many people are emotional at this sensitive time in Nigeria. Some are killing Nigerians out of emotions; others hate those who are killing them because of intolerance or greed.

Can Nigeria move away from these limiting factors and make real progress as a nation and become the greatest black nation on earth?

Religious bodies often talk of good or bad. It follows that there is nothing in between. You are either a sinner, or you are not. There is nothing like a little bit of sin. Walking outside religion, one can wonder if we can have a continuum, where some things can be extremely bad on one end and others are extremely good on the other end. This implies that some things can be neutral or somewhere within the continuum.

The other question I want us to examine is this: Are there things that are universally good or bad? Somehow it seems the answer depends on who is assessing. In other words, many individuals and groups will easily consider what benefits them as good, even when such is harmful to others, while they will see what is harmful to them as bad. We all know that everyone will do all they can to eliminate whatever harms or threatens his or her well-being. That process of elimination will be considered a good thing by that individual but a bad thing by the victim. It follows too that while we will be happy to consider killing a snake or mosquito a good thing, the snake and the mosquito will consider it an evil act.

By nature, human beings have strong instincts for survival, for growth, and to dominate their environment. People with excessive intensity of such instincts will tend to exhibit negative emotions like desire to enslave others, intimidation, oppression, greed, selfishness, jealousy, domineering tendencies, aggressiveness, heartlessness, meanness, and so on. Even as believers of a religion of love (Christianity)—which teaches us to love God and humankind, to avoid revenge, to always forgive, and to love our enemies—such persons will have a tendency to do bad things and then rationalize their actions.

If people tend to look at themselves as the reference point to decide what is good or bad, are there things that can be universally good or bad? While human beings tend to be selfish, God is good, and anything about God is therefore good. Any instruction from the God of love is good. Loving, caring, parenting, mentoring, and such are good. So killing, stealing, destruction, violence, and so forth are bad.

Let's say that individuals decide for themselves what benefits them and want to encourage the same for the good of all. Now let's say these individuals handed over some of their independence (their security, for example) as the price of communal living and, by extension, the good of all and civilized governance. It follows that laws are made for the good of the society, and so laws are good. Laws are modified or changed as things change or new revelations come into the open. Similarly, the laws of the God of love are good. Jesus Christ is the epitome of love and goodness. Anything that preaches hatred, killing, intolerance, and the like is, therefore, bad.

Are there good and bad things in this world? My opinion is that there are things that are good, and others are bad.

When we are having negative emotions like anger, envy, jealousy, resentment, disgust, and hatred, we tend not to appreciate the achievements, good gestures, and successes of the target of our emotions. We look for justifications to play such successes down and/or look for faults to justify why an achievement is a fluke or not worth celebrating. Human beings tend not to be happy when their perceived enemies make progress. They would prefer to have made the progress or been the recipient of luck themselves. Our judgments are impaired, and we sometimes even refuse help from such a person. That is, our emotions sometimes keep us down in the valley.

We should always be aware of these tendencies and be careful of decisions we make when we are in such states because we get sentimental and act in ways that, in the long run, affect us badly.

As explained earlier, emotions impede our sense of good judgement. The three main qualities of the mind are thought, memory, and emotions. Clearly, a good thinker will be intelligent, while someone with good memory will be clever and an overly emotional person may be foolish though not necessarily stupid.

An intelligent person may be innovative and a solution provider, while someone who has strong memory ability can replay events that happened many years ago as if they happened today, the same way a computer can remember. An emotional person can use this tendency positively for good, like being in love or being patriotic, while others can use it negatively and destructively.

If the brain has these three qualities (thought, memory, and emotions), then it follows that the three qualities can exist in different dominant levels and in different combinations in different people. That again can account for why we are different and why we react differently than others do to the same situation.

Example elucidating the possible various interactive outcomes of the qualities of the mind

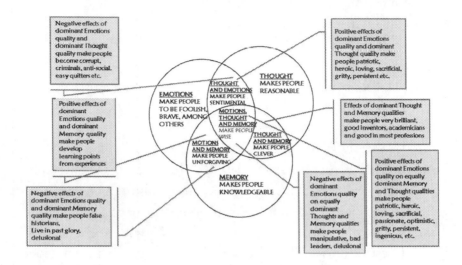

Fig. 7.1: **Qualities of the mind and various interactive outcomes.**

Kindly allow me to use an example to further elucidate this concept. We had a civil war in Nigeria, and during that war, many Igbos suffered. Many died of hunger. If there is another threat of war, the reactions of people will differ, depending on which of the qualities is dominant in them. How that civil war experience and the possibility of reliving another war affect Igbos will depend on these mental qualities:

- Those with high memory quality will remember exactly and vividly how they suffered as if it just happened yesterday. They will remember how they managed to survive the war. They will want to rely on their experience to survive.
- Those with high thought quality may not remember how exactly they managed to survive the war but will be able to think of new ways of surviving another war. What they can remember about the past war may not be reliable, but they can ruminate on the little they can remember.

- Those with strong emotional quality may remember what happened and how people died, but they will react variably depending on which emotion is dominant in them:
  - o Some may be so proud and so angry that they would want the war to commence immediately, even when they know many suffered and died during the previous war. To such people, a man must live standing up or die rather than stoop low, and they prefer death to allowing people to trample on them.
  - o Others may be so afraid that they would prefer to be slaves in the new dispensation than for many to die again.
  - o Some may be so consumed with love that they will actively work to prevent the war and avert loss of lives.

Reactions of people will be many depending on which of the several emotions is dominant in them.

- Apart from the examples given above, there will be others with both dominant thought and memory qualities. These people will not only appreciate the impact of the first war on them, as they can vividly remember everything, they will also be effective in actively proffering solutions, since they know where it pinches and why it should not pinch again. The advantage they have over those who can reason effectively but cannot remember the extent of the havoc experienced in the previous war is that they will put in more effort to prevent another war, since they clearly remember what happened the last time.
- It is important to know that anyone with dominant emotional quality will continue to suffer faulty judgement as a result of the prevailing emotions he or she experiences.
- Where emotions are not controlled, judgement will always be poorly made, but where emotions are controlled and targeted to solving problems in an individual who is also having effective thought and memory qualities is a wise and valuable person.

A wise person will commence problem solving immediately after the first war, so that same experience will not be relived if another war takes place. He or she will put in place mitigating measures that, if another war is inevitable, will reduce the suffering. A wise person is proactive and does not call for a war he or she will lose because doing so would be foolishness.

7.3 Conservatism, Progressivism, and Lovers of Change

- Change for the sake of change, like fashion, has no real productive value. Sometimes change brings about societal retrogression and deterioration of values. Change that is embedded in continuous improvement of standards and quality is progressive. So do not tell me to change. Show me the value the change will bring, about and I shall become an apostle for that change.

Let us hypothetically place people into three groups with regards to the ease with which they accept change—conservatives, those who love change, and progressives.

Each group has a vital role to play in societal advancement and culture formation. Conservatives ensure stability, while change lovers ensure that risks, which may eventually bring about societal advancement, are taken. And the progressives are the leaders who manage the process, so that only changes that will bring about improvement are taken, while stability is maintained. They ensure there is no radical departure from those qualities, culture, or tradition that make that group distinct.

The change lovers are easily bored, restless, and impatient. They want things to change from time to time. They are in love with fashion and will adopt any new trend without considering its merits. They may take unnecessary risks just to have change. They would destroy the 'old' rather than build on it as the progressives do. These people are highly disliked by the conservatives. The conservatives also dislike the progressives because they, too, would like change, so long as that change will result in improvement in the relevant circumstance.

The conservatives fear change; they want the status quo to always remain the same. They do not want to take risks because risk has the probability that failure may occur, and they fear failure, especially if the status quo favours them. (They ask, why change a winning horse?) To them, failure is shameful or embarrassing, an end in itself, and without a learning element. The conservatives do not want to venture out of their comfort zones, and in organizations, they form pressure groups to resist change. The level of resistance will depend on the source of the idea. If the idea does not come from their camp, then the resistance will be fierce.

Progressives like our Lord Jesus Christ, Socrates, Reverend Martin Luther King, Isaac Newton, and Isaac Adaka-Boro, among others had ideas that were more advanced than those of the generations they were born in. And their ideas were resisted violently.

If we had never changed in the past, we would have continued to kill twins to this day, for example. As Christians, we would have refused to use the airplane because our Lord Jesus Christ never used it. That is not to say that, like the 'change lovers', we should keep changing for the sake of change. If we did so, how would we retain those idiosyncrasies—traditions, customs, and cultures—that give our societies or organizations their distinct identities?

However, we need to be open-minded. To solve problems, we must think outside the box, and we must embrace new ideas that have potential to move us to the next positive level. If we fail, then fine. Failure is a learning process, which is an essential requirement for eventual success.

Let us know that any society or organization that resists change by all means also insists on stagnation and eventual decline by any means.

I have always said that it takes courage and is a good strategy to admit wrong and change direction quickly before a policy decision causes an unintended harm. Nobody, especially a new government, can be a repository of all the best practices or knowledge in every field of national governance. Every human being makes mistakes, and the beauty is we can own up to such mistakes in time and make amendments before it is too late. Perfect quality management always is too idealistic an expectation, especially in non-exact sciences like macroeconomics and national governance, where at every turn, several factors come into play and should be considered before decisions are made.

I agree that every government should endeavour not to have frequent policy somersaults or what some people call flip-flop management system, if competent persons are put in the right places. However, when changes are needed because of changing circumstances or mistakes made, we should commence damage control or mitigating measures immediately. In national government, it is impossible not to have some politicians manning some key positions. However, the leader must be wise as to how he or she selects the people who will oversee sensitive positions that are critical factors in the achievement of his or her goals and aspirations. Politicians are sometimes not only competent for specialized offices requiring expertise management but also in possession of agendas that run contrary to the avowed goals of the government.

Governance at the national level does not need trial and error or idealistic aides who are theoretical but cannot put much policy into practice. What is needed is the engagement of well-tested experts who will not make avoidable and costly mistakes that will affect millions of Nigerians and cost equally huge sums of national fund. Leaders and their aides must be realistic thinkers who are not narrow-minded and are able to 'think outside of the box'—people who look at problems from many perspectives before decisions are made.

A word of caution however: Nigeria is a big project. Failure affects more than 180 million Nigerians and many more investors from outside this nation. We, therefore, do not want those in power who are not prepared or will never be prepared—whether that be because of an inherent lack of capacity or because they are strongly affected by emotions—as they will drag everyone down a negative path.

7.4 Developing Good Mass Conscience and Democratic Principles

Democracy encourages mediocrity. Do not get offended because that is the truth. It seeks to establish as law the choices and decisions of the majority of the population. However, majority decisions statistically tend towards the median or middle positions in population distributions. In such normal data, there is the tendency for the majority to gravitate towards the middle. The excellent or expert opinions and the stupid or uninformed opinions are usually at either extreme of the distribution curve.

Democratic decisions are therefore not often the worst or the best opinions on any matter but because they were decisions taken by the majority of the people with the inputs from all, they often tend to be robust and by that I mean they are often not the very worse decisions to be taken except when the choices are few and emotions take a major role in the decision making. Equally, their negative consequences do not cause major upheavals. Often the population tolerate the inconveniences grudgingly and quietly because they made the decision.

Democratic decisions, though not perfect, can be further improved if there is aggressive education and debate prior to the time such decisions are made, so that, as much as possible, people are given the opportunity to make informed decisions. That is to say, education is a way to reduce to a bearable level the population of ignorant decision makers. Just like any good technology, education and debates can be misused and abused. People can be fed with lies, indoctrinated, and misinformed with the sole aim of deceiving the populace into accepting wrong information or buying into malicious propaganda designed to benefit crooked politicians. Many times, politicians that call others corrupt are worse.

Despite these shortcomings of democratic decision-making, decisions made democratically nonetheless remain better decisions than those taken within the context of dictatorship, fear, intimidation, and the like, where public input is not sought, experts are not consulted, and collaborative efforts are not encouraged. Therefore, democracy is still the best. Let us keep discussing it and improving on it.

Every democratic nation has, from time to time, an opportunity to choose from a set of candidates who should lead them politically. In Nigeria and America, this selection process takes place every four years. We also choose leaders for the lower levels of government and not just for the national government.

Every citizen has a duty to give his or her input in this process, and we are allowed to advocate for our preferred candidates in a civilized manner. Most times, choices are made based on certain individual considerations. Some tend towards sentimentality, while others try to be objective. In all, however, people tend to be very emotive, and longstanding relationships are sometimes irreparably damaged because of political differences.

I am human, and I have my own baggage. My assessment of candidates, though, is often based on objective criteria, mainly on the relative competencies and suitability of the candidates. I also consider some other emotional issues, like who is tolerant to others in terms of religion, ethnicity, race, background, and the like. By implication, I get emotional, and my fair judgment of some candidates—who I perceive to dislike my people because of my religion, ethnicity, or other group I belong to—is clouded. For me, considering that as one of the factors is still being objective because I will not support a candidate who will, in some way, enslave or oppress my people.

For those of us who are not active politicians and who do not belong to any political party in Nigeria, our assessment in terms of which political party and individual to vote should depend on the competencies and suitability of the candidates The relative competencies of the available candidates is what we should consider important because the bottom line in governance is who is a better leader who will improve the lot of the masses. Often the system throws up candidates who are not the very best in the society, and our choices should be based on the best available.

This is why some advocate for independent candidates. One day, we may be so politically aware that even a poor independent candidate can be funded by the Nigerian people as a whole to win elections.

When the parties change or their candidates change, we reassess because we have no permanent friends or enemies in politics. All we have is permanent collective interests as a people.

The dilemma many face is what to do when they know that their choice is not likely to win an election. They wonder in such circumstances whether they should give their vote to the candidate who will likely win or whether they should, as a matter of principle, vote in line with the dictates of their consciences. Some might think this is a small issue, but many find this dilemma stressful. For me, however, everyone must be principled; we must always vote according to our consciences in terms of the candidates' competencies, suitability to perform well, and which party will protect our collective interest as a people.

Everybody in Nigeria and even in the developed nations like the United States of America should discount the idea of states traditionally belonging to one party or the other. What is important is the leadership and political direction of a party. What the common man needs is not his tribe's man becoming president or governor. What the common man wants is the president or governor who will improve his quality of life, provide him employment, provide social amenities, and give him a sense of belonging.

7.5 Good Leadership for National Advancement

Nigeria needs a political party that is built on discipline, fairness, justice, equity, patriotism, and nonviolent progressivism. We are in a democracy, where the collective decisions of the party are superior to the choices of its leaders. Nigeria needs to make progress to claim its pride of place in the comity of nations.

We need good leadership in our nation.

- Nigeria can't be called big for nothing. We are big for something. Our vast and talented human resource is something. And our abundant natural resources can count for something. Nothing can hinder a nation dedicated and desirous to win. All we need is good leadership in every sector to help us.

- There can't be good leadership without good followership. Progressive citizenship comes with good companionship. Let us all do something to end this pervasive hardship. Encouraging tolerance will enhance friendship. All we need is good leadership in every sector to help us.

- The conflicts we have had should have made us better—if we had tried win-win solutions and learned from each other. It is now time to look inwards and much deeper. The divisive factors are less than those bringing us together. All we need is good leadership in every sector to help us.

- There was a time roads were in good condition always. Improve transportation and end these endless delays. Now our railways are in a mess, and so are the airways. Leaders should commence improvement without delays. All we need is good leadership in every sector to help us.

- Political wickedness makes the people hopeless. So many are helpless due to leadership selfishness. Don't be compassionless; show the people some kindness. Don't be emotionless; give someone true happiness. All we need is good leadership in every sector to help us.

- We cannot stop talking about vices like corruption. But it can be managed if the rule of law is in action. All forms of discrimination are aberrations for condemnation. Let us eliminate corruption and stop discrimination so that we are not left behind by civilization. All we need is good leadership in every sector to help us.

- Impunity brings about adversity, hostility, and calamity. Charity enhances prosperity, peace, and unity. Don't take for granted the indivisibility of our country. It is good we know that impossibility is not a reality. All we need is good leadership in every sector to help us.

- Let us work hard and obtain new technologies. Let us, for posterity, regain our past glories. Ours may still be a giant among some African countries. We need to be stronger with our complementary diversities. All we need is good leadership in every sector to help us.

Most leaders in Africa will not peacefully relinquish power, even in insignificant settings like social clubs, community groups, or other smaller groups. The 'stay put syndrome' gets more pronounced as the benefits that accrue to the leadership increase. Examples where this phenomenon is very rampant include local government, state government, and national leadership positions. It is also rampant in community and social club settings.

It is rare to find people like Nelson Mandela (former president of South Africa) who will peacefully and happily step down from lucrative leadership positions. Those are positions that are lucrative even when the leader is not corrupt and has no plan to exploit his position for his selfish interest. While people like Mandela are scarce in Africa, the reverse seems to be the situation in many developed societies because of the sustainable and strong institutions that have been put in place.

In Nigeria and in most African nations, people will try even when it is impossible to attempt to rule as long as they have life in them. You cannot expect a leader not to seek re-election, no matter how poor the leader's health is, so long as the individual is able to stand and make campaign speech for at least four minutes. That is how bad this syndrome is.

Apart from the lucrativeness of the offices, fear that the next leader may choose to prosecute them for bad governance or corrupt acts plays a role in leaders attempting to stay put. Such leaders decide therefore to avoid prosecution is to remain in office for life.

Another factor that motivates such people to take this option is their knowledge that many of our people are sycophants. The leaders know that some people would sell their consciences and even their families for a piece of cake. Some Nigerians do not really care about good governance and effective performance as a basis for re-electing a leader. The key factors we consider for political re-election are which of the candidates will take care of our own individual and selfish interests and which of the candidates is closest to us in terms of ethnicity and religious affiliations.

We do not care about how the leader has managed the economy, whether the leader was fair to all, and whether the leader met past promises made to the electorate. No, we will even rationalize on behalf of the leader as to why he did not perform well. We will be ready to kill for the leader, and we will be ready to destroy the nation if we do not have our way.

Nigeria has a long way to go before we can join the league of politically developed nations. We have been a promising nation as long as we can remember. Many economic analysts predicted Nigeria to be in the group of next emerging powerful nations, and often the rest in that group have moved forward, leaving Nigeria going the opposite direction. A number of nations that did not have the quality of human resources, natural agricultural potential, and mineral deposit endowment have overtaken us in the quest for continued national advancement.

It is for these reasons that we have remained largely a beggar nation, when we are well endowed and positioned for greatness. For a very long time, many nations have come to us to exploit us in furtherance of their own interests. This has been so from the era of slavery through to the eras of colonialism and neocolonialism. Currently, people exploit us, and we smile sheepishly in gratitude because we have not been able to install good leaders. Even if we try, will our exploiters allow the good leaders to stay if such leaders prevent further exploitation? Our leaders have no interest in those things that will benefit all the people and result in rapid national advancement. They are only after the satisfaction of their selfish and ethnic interests.

We must wake up from our deep slumber before we can make good progress. Sentimentality is the bane of our rapid advancement, and we cannot be effectively rational, objective, and result focused as long as all our judgement is tainted with sentiments. We have been a sleeping giant in Africa, and if we continue to wallow in our slumber, then we shall drift into stupor forever.

7.6 Love as an Overarching Concept for National Advancement

Humankind in its primitive state would rather fight an opponent who disagrees, rather than try to reason with that opponent; a community and a nation would prefer to start a war with another community or nation that has a disagreement with it than to understand the stance of that would-be opponent. That way, it is the most powerful in any conflict that has its way and not the party that justly should win. The world believes in jungle justice, and no one resists as those who are powerful capture, enslave, or kill to their hearts' desire. Among the organisms, we human beings are the worst offenders in terms of killing our own kind for no just reason.

Among all living things, human beings are also the most intelligent. Humankind has transformed the earth so much that it is, in every sense, a disadvantage to all others that coexist with humanity on earth. Our selfishness is so profound that we are not only selfish to other beings but also to our own kind. So long as that individual person gains from a thing, no matter how unjust it is, it is all right. For humankind, all is fair as long as we are advantaged, and all is unfair and against collective interest as long as we are individually disadvantaged.

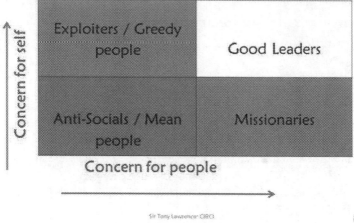

Inter-relating concerns for self and others

Fig. 7.2: **An illustration of how concerns for self and others interrelate.**

The illustration in figure 7.2 shows that good leaders must have concern for those they lead as well as for themselves. Other combinations result in different types of leaders. Leaders whose concern for others matches their concern for their own personal needs (see the top right quadrant) will be effective at understanding the problems of followers and relating those problems to their own.

Those who do not care about their own needs but only how to satisfy the followers and making sacrifices for others will be exploited. Such a person is like a missionary (see the bottom right quadrant).

Those who have no concern for either their needs or those of the followers (bottom left quadrant) are dangerous leaders. They can easily drive everyone insane or even enter into unnecessary wars just because of pride or other negative qualities.

Finally, those who are interested only in helping themselves with disregard for others (top left quadrant) are exploiters and are not good leaders.

Human beings are the only religious animals, and yet humankind is very devilish and rationalizes. We believe in God, but we encourage slavery. We are very religious, but there is among us a great deal of criminality. We suppress the minority, we steal their resources, and we justify our actions with phony pedantic justifications. It is only humankind that can take mineral oil belonging to another and give good justification why it must be so and even justify why the owners should be killed if they resist.

Human beings have developed and manufactured weapons of mass destruction, so much so that humanity is the very likely threat that will end life on earth, with our philosophy of mutually assured destruction.

Like all other animals, we eat, we feel emotions, we procreate, we grow, and we eventually die. Yet we feel we are superior. Are we superior in intelligence or foolishness? I'd bet the answer is both.

Let all humankind know that, if we want to live forever, we have to love God; other human beings; and all other animals, plants, and microorganisms. Let all humankind know that, if we have to live forever, we have to use our intelligence to support our creator and not to antagonize Him.

Let all humankind know that we are all made equal. No human being is superior to the other, and when we die, we shall all disintegrate the same way. The concept of superiority is vanity, and so a king or prince today may be a slave tomorrow if the circumstances change. A landlord today may be a tenant or a destitute person tomorrow if circumstances change.

In heaven, our earthly wealth will mean nothing because it is actually nothing. You came to this world without a thing, and so you shall go back.

Are human beings actually superior to other animals? I don't know indeed, though I'll ask that you permit me, as a Christian, to refer to the Bible, which says that humankind was created in the image of God. That image obviously has nothing to do with our body, our intelligence, and our earthly makeup. That image must be spiritual. But unfortunately, that spiritual image is dead in most human beings.

The search for true love is an elusive concept that is not achievable if it is expected that such love must be mutually shared by the partners. The simple reason is that it is difficult to find someone you have near perfect love for who will have similar near perfect love for you.

In reality, falling in love is a choice after a process of judgement based on practical issues and in line with exigencies. Sometimes, love is spontaneous, wild, and compelling. But in the end, some judgement is made for its sustainability.

Based on the above, does true love exist?

I will say that it does—if one accepts the premise that you can love without the expectation of reciprocity. If that premise is accepted, then it is possible and some people have experienced true love. True love is unconditional, targeted towards an object of love that may not even merit it. It is all about sacrifice and more sacrifice. True love does not demand anything in return. Many times, true love is triggered by sympathy or the desire to help the object of love. And sometimes, too, the object of love becomes exploitative and fraudulently takes things from the one who is in love. This can complicate the life of the one who is in love, who may choose not to be vulnerable in the future. So, in giving, it is good to give what you can sacrifice and be happy that you had the opportunity to touch another's life. Do not worry about the underlying motive for a favour requested. Only follow your heart and thank God for the opportunity to have touched someone's life.

Perfect true love is an idealistic concept, and only few persons, like Jesus Christ, can enjoy and have enjoyed that kind of experience. For many human beings, true love will remain an elusive concept throughout life, the pursuit of which preoccupies many people.

How does love affect us as Nigerians in terms of contributing towards making this nation the best nation in the world?

Nigeria is the only nation we can truly call home, where you will not be considered a second-class citizen by anyone deliberately or by mistake. It is the nation we shall bequeath to our generations yet unborn.

This is the basis of governance and peaceful coexistence for sustainable advancement in Nigeria.

Conclusion

Nations, states, and communities are encouraging and attracting internal and external investors. However, some elements in Nigeria and South Africa, for example, are chasing away investors or people they perceive to be different from themselves or to be taking their businesses and jobs, without realizing that these same strangers contribute greatly to the vibrancy of their economies. If you chase away people of any race or tribe, it is every one of that tribe that will go, and they will leave with their transferable assets.

Such mass movement in any nation or parts of any nation will result in massive and prolonged recession that will compound the situation for which the xenophobia or 'ethno-phobia' started in the first place.

The solution to economic difficulty is not to scare away investments and make the situation pathetic. Rather, it is to encourage more investment with well-thought-through investment policies.

The impact of mass movement of economically active people from a state or a region is massive. This happened during the Nigerian Civil War when many Southerners left the North. The economy crashed.

If many leave a location, who will rent the accommodations?

Who will patronize the businesses?

Who will pay the taxes?

Some who teach in the universities and work in the hospitals will leave too.

Those who introduce variation and competition in the university classrooms as students leave too.

The implication is secondary recession.

7.7 The Impact of Sustainable Development, Corruption, and Leadership on Rapid National Development (Graphical Presentation)

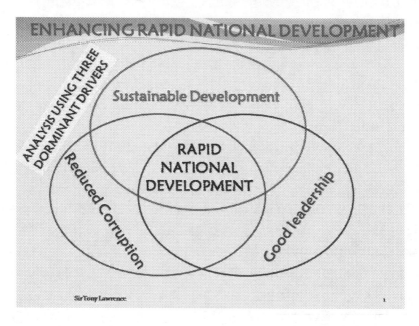

Fig. 7.3: **Sustainable development, reduced corruption, and good leadership as critical drivers for rapid national development.**

In figure 7.3, factors that are important for rapid national development have been simplified to consider only the three most dominant/critical drivers at each level of analysis. At the first level of rapid national development in this particular scenario, the critical drivers identified for rapid national development are good leadership, reduced corruption, and sustainable development.

The assumption is that, in nature, though several numerous factors influence every outcome that is seen, their effects on the subject differ. And usually only about 20 per cent of the factors impacting any subject accounts for 80 per cent of the impact or resultant effect.

So, this drill-down analysis that I've developed considers only the three factors that are perceived to be most critical to understanding the phenomenon. The analysis will continue for another two steps before a holistic proposal for intervention proposed. In this case, rapid national development is used, in line with the focus of this book.

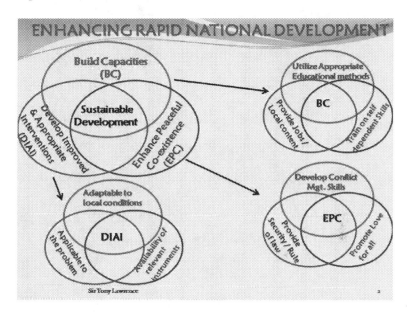

Fig. 7.4: **Utilization of sustainable development components for national development.**

The illustration in figure 7.4 explains the utilization of the three-priority factor drill-down analysis for the sustainable development component of the rapid national development analysis found in figure 7.3.

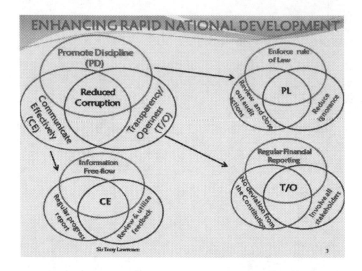

Fig. 7.5: **Utilization of reduced corruption components for national development.**

The illustration in figure 7.5 explains the utilization of the three-priority factor drill-down analysis for reduced the corruption component of the rapid national development analysis found in figure 7.3.

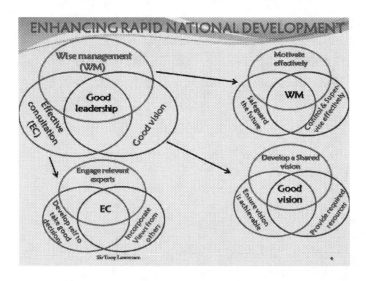

Fig. 7.6: **Utilization of good leadership components for national development**

The illustration in figure 7.6 explains the utilization of the three-priority factor drill-down analysis for the good leadership component in the rapid national development analysis found in figure 7.3.

This prioritized drill-down analysis for factors that affect any situation is a better way of setting effective objectives from set goals towards achieving those goals. The first step becomes the goal, the next drill-down becomes the main objective, and subsequent drill-down will represent unit objectives or activities depending on the level of depth required.

References

Leonard, Arthur Glyn (2009), *The Lower Niger and Its Tribes* (BiblioBazaar, LLC), 21–22.

Jones, G. I. (2001), *The Trading States of the Oil Rivers: A Study of Political Development in Eastern Nigeria* (James Currey Publishers), 15ff, ISBN 0-85255-918-6.

Darah, Godini G. (2017), "Democracy and Development in Nigeria: The Case Study of Rivers State," Lecture delivered on the occasion of Rivers State Golden Jubilee Celebration.

http://anthonywakwelawrence.com/

http://www.cracong.org/supreme-court-upholds-right-of-female-child-to-inherit-properties-in-igboland/

https://www.facebook.com/Anthony Wakwe Lawrence

http://www.circi-ngo.org/

http://www.eajournals.org/journals/international-journal-of-development-and-economic-sustainability-ijdes/vol-5-issue-5-september-2017/sustainability-filters-enhancers-towards-improving-intervention-functionality-sustainable-advancement-holistic-concept/

http://edition.cnn.com/2017/07/11/world/sutter-mass-extinction-ceballos-study/index.htmlhttps://www.google.com.ng/search?q=who+life+expectancy+by+country&oq=who+life+exppectancy&aqs=chrome.1.69i57j0l5.17028j0j4&sourceid=chrome&ie=UTF-8

http://www.nigerialocal.com.ng/complete-list-ethnic-groups-nigeria/ 371 ethnic groups

http://www.ng.undp.org/content/nigeria/en/home/post-2015/sdg-overview.html

https://www.quora.com/What-is-Triple-Filter-test-of-Socrates

http://www.vanguardngr.com/2009/06/ogoni-9-ogoni-4-and-june-12-prologue/

http://www.worldometers.info/world-population/nigeria-population/

Ihebuzor, N. A. (2015), https://visionvoiceandviews.com/2015/04/22/ramblings-and-jottings-on-corruption/

——, http://noelihebuzor.tumblr.com/post/20111927449/ramblings-and-jottings-on-corruption-by-noel

——, https://visionvoiceandviews.com/2013/04/13/needed-fast-but-fair-prosecution-of-persons-with-corruption-charges/

Boesler, Matthew (2013), The Population of Nigeria Is Set to Overtake That of the US by 2045,' *Business Insider*, 8 Aug.

Shaw, T., and Daniells, S. G. H. (1984), 'Excavations At Iwo-Eleru, Ondo State, Nigeria', *West African Journal of Archaeology*.

Sule, Abubakar (2014), "The Archaeology of Northern Nigeria: Trade, People and Polities, 1500 BP Onwards," *Azania* 49/4 (8 Dec.)

World Health Organization (WHO) (2016) in *This Day*, 10 December

United Nations World Commission on Environment and Development (1987), *Our Common Future.*

UNDP in Nigeria (2016), "2030 Agenda for Sustainable Development), http://www.ng.undp.org/content/nigeria/en/home/post-2015/sdg-overview.html.

About the Author

Sir Anthony Wakwe Lawrence has worked in several organizations. He was a teacher and later a vice principal (1983–1988), a research officer with Rivers State Agricultural Development Programme (ADP) (1988), a research associate with International Institute of Tropical Agriculture (IITA) (1988–1991) and sustainable community development/public relations staff with Shell Petroleum Development Company of Nigeria Limited (SPDC) (1991–2008).

From 2008 onwards, Lawrence became the chairman of Community Inter-Relations and Conciliation Initiative (CIRCI) a non-governmental organization (NGO) that carries out sustainable community development and public relations activities on its own and in collaboration with other partners for communities. He has personally served as consultant to many private and governmental organizations.

Lawrence obtained a Bachelor of Science in biological sciences at the University of Lagos (1982), a Master of Arts in philosophy in crop production at Rivers State University of Science and Technology (1988), a postgraduate diploma (PGD) in management sciences from the Rivers State University of Science and Technology (1997) and a Master of Business Administration (MBA) from Abubakar Tafawa Balewa University, Bauchi State (2002).

He has also attended several on-the-job trainings in the United States, the United Kingdom, Tanzania, Swaziland, Kenya, and Nigeria.

Sir Anthony Wakwe Lawrence is a Knight of St. Christopher in the Church of Nigeria—Anglican Communion. A native of Abonnema and Aboh in Nigeria, he is married and has five children. He was born on 2 February 1959 and speaks Kalabari and English fluently.

Printed in the United States
By Bookmasters